# CUNNINGLY DEVISED FABLES

# Cunningly Devised Fables

## PAUL YOUNG

**B. McCALL BARBOUR**
28 GEORGE IV BRIDGE
EDINBURGH EH1 1ES, SCOTLAND

**JOHN RITCHIE LTD**
CHRISTIAN PUBLICATIONS

40 Beansburn, Kilmarnock, Scotland

ISBN 1 904064 12 4

Copyright © 2002 by John Ritchie Ltd.
40 Beansburn, Kilmarnock, Scotland

Typeset by John Ritchie Ltd., Kilmarnock
Printed by Bell & Bain Ltd., Glasgow

# Contents

# Preface

Over a number of years I have gathered information on many religious cults and this overview presents some of the material collected. The first section describes some general features which characterise many of the cults, this is then followed by a summary of the history, beliefs and practices of the more widely known groups.

Today the word "cult" is considered by some to be derogatory and prejudicial and there is a tendency to replace it with the term "new religious movement". Whatever form of words are used it is a sad fact that many people have testified of the damage which a cult has done to their family life, marriage relationship, personality or tranquility of mind. Some have been so disturbed as to commit suicide. Many bear the wounds of damaged emotions and the scars of psychological problems many years after they have left the particular cult to which they once belonged. One lady, three years after leaving the Moonies, said: "It is hard, even now, to say that I have recovered fully, because there are parts of the experience that will go with me forever." The horror and pain that lie behind her words can almost be felt.

It is impossible to give too many warnings, as clearly there are serious dangers with many cults. They need to be avoided at all costs and especially so by young people. Young people are energetic, enthusiastic, idealistic and want to change the world. Unfortunately there are too many cults led by strong personalities who prey upon such qualities, often for personal gain and to the detriment of the young people concerned.

Paul Young

# Introduction

Freedom of belief is a fundamental human right and people are entitled to believe whatever religious idea they consider suitable and to join any religious organization they so desire. However it is also our right to examine religious beliefs and to ascertain whether such may be harmful or damaging and whether they are based on truth or clear foundational evidence. It is also our right to issue warnings when such beliefs are at variance with the Bible and to encourage people to a straightforward acceptance of the Christian Gospel as outlined in Holy Scripture and which gives the blessing of eternal life and forgiveness of sins through Jesus Christ our Lord.

## Definition of a Cult

A Christian cult is a group of people who gather around someone's particular interpretation of the Bible. It is usually characterized by a major deviation from orthodox Christian teaching and by a contradiction of the truths of historical Christianity. The deviation usually relates to the person of the Lord Jesus Christ and often His deity is denied.

## Do Cults Prosper?

The obvious answer to this is Yes. Millions of people have been deceived by a cult, believing that they have found the answer to their deepest need. Very often their lives have been taken over and they choose to relinquish all major decisions, yielding them to their religious leaders. Such decisions may be: whom to marry, what to do with money, where to live, what job to take, whether to vote and for whom.

The Mormons have grown from 30 members in 1830 to over 8 million today, while the Jehovah's Witnesses have millions of members worldwide. It is estimated that there are 500 cults in Britain with about half a million members and over 3,000 cults in America with over 3 million members.

Cults prosper because they seem to have the answers to life's deep needs, and also offer total life alternatives to the materialism and rat race mentality of the western world. They initially offer friendship, kindness and community to people who may be lonely, hurt or sad. This so often comes across as the opposite of the hard, harsh indifference of orthodox established churches.

# Characteristics of Cults

## Alternative Sources of Authority

Christianity has one source of authority and that is the Holy Bible, consisting of sixty-six books, divided into two sections known as the Old and New Testaments. For Christians the Bible is the final and complete revelation of God to man and is the sole guide in matters of belief and practice.

Cults have often formulated extra sources for authority which usually in their eyes supersede the Bible. These take the form of written statements or verbal pronouncements from the cult leaders. The Moonies accept *Divine Principle* as the new revelation from God. This book written by the Rev. Moon is effectively more highly thought of by Moonies than the Bible. This is also true of Mormons who look to the *Book of Mormon* as their special revelation from God. The Children of God considered the Mo letters as authoritative, while Jehovah's Witnesses look to the writings of Taze Russell, their founder, as the new revelation from God.

It is generally true to say that these writings often contradict Scripture and deny the cardinal truths of the Gospel. They may also be self-contradictory and internally inconsistent. Jehovah's Witnesses have gone so far as to write their own version of the Bible to incorporate their particular doctrines.

## New Interpretations of Scripture

Cults have a tendency to reinterpret Scripture and give it a meaning that is far removed from what it says in context and from what historical Christianity has always accepted. The cult leader or leaders may state that they now have the key that unlocks the truth of Scripture. They suggest that this key to understanding Scripture has always been hidden until they were given it by the grace of God.

One obvious example is that of the Jehovah's Witnesses who have reinterpreted the passages which ban the drinking of blood and given them a medical meaning that bans blood transfusions even if loss of life is the result. This is both a travesty of Biblical interpretation and a callous approach to the value of human life.

## Denial of Essential Christian Truths

It is usual for the cults to deny fundamental truths of the historic Christian faith. Often the Trinity of God is denied, and consequently the deity of Christ and the deity and personality of the Holy Spirit. The work of atonement of Christ when He died for our sins on the cross is denied. This is often seen by cults as simply an example of martyrdom, a failure, a mistake or just irrelevant. heaven and hell, a literal devil, the fall of mankind into sin and even sin itself is often denied.

## Changing Theology

Cults do not necessarily have a standard unchanging theology. They adapt and change their teaching to suit the times in which they live. These changes are often dressed up as new revelation from God, and would never be admitted as correction of past mistakes.

Mormons have had to change their teaching on polygamy and the acceptance of Negro members. Jehovah's Witnesses have changed their teaching on the use of vaccinations for the prevention of disease as well as pronouncements on the Second Coming of Christ.

## False Prophecy

Cults are in the habit of making prophetic statements and still they continue to flourish even when the prophecy fails to come true. The Jehovah's Witnesses have predicted the date of the Second Coming of Christ on a number of occasions and each one has been proved erroneous. Herbert Armstrong, founder of the Worldwide Church of God, prophesied that drought, famine and disease would kill millions in the U.S.A. four years from when he made his pronouncement in 1967. It failed to happen.

The Bible says: "When a prophet speaketh in the name of the LORD, if the thing follow not, nor come to pass, that is the thing which the LORD hath not spoken, but the prophet hath spoken it presumptuously: thou shalt not be afraid of him." (Deuteronomy 18.22). Clearly in the light of this Biblical statement false prophecies indicate false cults.

## Salvation Through Works

Cults deny that salvation and acceptance with God is on the basis of faith and faith alone. They deny the Biblical truth of justification by faith. They add to the doctrine of grace. Usually, the cult will say "do this"; "work hard"; "give enough"; "attend our meetings" and you may be saved and enjoy eternal life. They hold out a hope and the members start on a never-ending treadmill to try and work their way to heaven and eternal life.

Members of a cult often have to give of their money, their time, their energy, and they have to attend meetings, study times, lectures, and retreats. At the end of all that there may be the possibility of eternal life. This gives a tenuous hope at best and at worse can lead to total disillusionment and alienation from God.

## Rejection of Historical Christianity

Cults generally denounce mainline churches as false or apostate, claiming that their own cult is now the true church or people of God. Helena Blavatsky, the founder of Theosophy, said: "Christianity is now a religion of arrogance a convenient screen for hypocrisy." While Joseph Smith founder of Mormons said: "I answered that I must join none of them (mainline churches) for they are all wrong". Many cults claim they have an exclusive right to the truth of God and all but themselves are suspect, false and wrong.

## Money

The founder of Scientology, Ron Hubbard, is supposed to have said as a young man, that the quickest way to make a million is to start a new religion. He certainly proved that to be true, as his estate was worth over £500 million on his death.

The Mormons have huge land holdings in Canada, the U.S.A. and Hawaii. They own hotel chains, the second largest financial institution west of Mississippi: the Beneficial Life Insurance Company, as well as hospitals, schools, televison and radio stations and a controlling interest in the Los Angeles Times. The Moonie empire is said to be worth over 5 billion dollars, while the Jehovah Witnesses made £3.3 million from literature selling in Britain alone, in 1984.

There is of course, nothing wrong with legitimate

business transactions and there is no implication of financial wrong doing, except in the case of the Rev. Moon who did an 18 month jail sentence in America for tax fraud. It is the means of acquiring the wealth which is controversial because so often it seems to be exploitation of the gullible.

Moonie recruits have to spend long hours every day on the streets selling literature, plastic flowers and button badges with all money going to the church's main funds. Recruits exist on little sleep and little food, they are expected to lie, deceive and resort to almost any means to make a sale or gain a donation. Thus many unsuspecting members of the general public have given a donation in the belief that it is going to some worthwhile charity, little realizing that it is going to the Moonies, otherwise known as the Unification Church.

Scientology is essentially a series of courses, which if followed will eventually bring the fullness of enlightenment, or so it is claimed. The courses don't come cheap, with each course costing more than the previous one, and to do the complete course will probably cost within the region of £150,000. Very few have done all the available courses.

Many cults urge their followers to give all their money to the religion, even to sell valuables and donate the proceeds to the cult. The result is an army of impoverished followers living in poor dormitory quarters, while the leaders live in luxury. The Rev. Moon lives in a mansion at a 22-acre estate in New York State. Bhagwan Shree Rajneesh lived in a mansion with a computer-controlled swimming pool, while his followers lived in cramped shacks and went on fund raising tours for him.

Everyone needs to be careful of a religion which

makes constant demands that its followers give money, make money, collect money and find money for the movement's coffers. Such a religion is not funding the work of God but the lifestyles of the leaders and founders of the cult.

## Sexual Impropriety

The Bible and historical Christianity have been very clear in the area of sexual relationships. The Bible emphasizes that we should abstain from such relationships before marriage and be faithful to one spouse within marriage. Deviations like homosexuality, lesbianism, relationships with children or animals are expressly condemned. Thus if a religion or its leaders teach and practice something other than what is taught in Scripture we see a clear violation of God's will.

The "Children of God" was a cult founded by David Berg, who later styled himself Moses "Mo" David. He had firm control over his followers and communicated to them by means of correspondence known as "Mo" letters. He encouraged his followers to seduce people into the movement. He termed his girls "Hookers for Jesus" and described their activities as "Flirty Fishing". He also encouraged homosexuality among his followers, sex with children, group sex and circulated pornographic videos. The AIDS epidemic, as well as negative publicity has curtailed much of this activity. The Mormons believed in and practiced polygamy in the early part of their history. They were forced to change their policy on this matter, at least in public, by pressure from the U.S. government. Bhagwam Shree Rajneesh suggested to his followers that a total lack of sexual inhibition would create divinity. He put great emphasis upon the sex act and his female followers regarded sex with Rajneesh as the pinnacle of their ambitions, being the closest they would get to true enlightenment.

Not all cults emphasize sexuality or encourage deviant or promiscuous sexual activity. But when the strictures of the Bible are ignored and disobeyed we are certainly dealing with something other than true Christianity.

**Power**

Some cults go beyond the desire to make money or give free expression to the leaders' sexual predilections. Some seek power, even the power to influence and indeed control governments.

One such example is the Unification Church (Moonies) whose avowed aims are political. The Moonies have maintained a strong anti-Communist stance and have supported right wing dictatorships including that of Argentina during the Falkland's conflict. They helped fund a coup in Bolivia and supported with volunteers and finances the right wing party of Jean Le Pen in France. The Rev. Moon has talked of members of his church serving as senators and congressmen in Washington D.C. so that he can influence the U.S.A. government. His prestigious newspaper *The Washington Times* is said to be one of the papers used by the U.S. President as part of his daily briefings. The Mormon church has great influence in the U.S. state of Utah and the Rajneesh followers tried to influence elections in the area of Oregon where they settled.

Money, sex and power can have tragic repercussions, as was the case with the Jonestown massacre in Guyana. A self-proclaimed Messiah known as the Rev. Jim Jones took a group of about a thousand followers and they built a community in the jungles of Guyana in South America. His control was total and eventually he induced over 900 of his followers to join him in a mass suicide. What was revealed subsequently was a sordid tale of a man given to paranoia, who revelled in his sexual exploits with his followers and who manipulated them for money, totally controlling their lives.

Not all cults show all the characteristics mentioned above. However all show some of these in one way or another. It is important that the Bible-believing Christian should learn to recognise the signs of a cult and not be deceived by the apparent friendliness of their missionaries, their Biblical sounding language or by their so called "new" knowledge. Many have found to their cost that it us much easier to join a cult than it is to leave that cult.

The critical examination of a religion's beliefs and practices is not wrong, especially where there could be danger both for adherents and for society at large. Recent events such as those involving David Koresh's followers at Waco, the Solar Temple religion in Switzerland and the so-called 'Toxic Terror' in Tokyo give great cause for concern and good reason for critical analysis of new religious movements.

# The Watchtower Bible and Tract Society (Jehovah's Witnesses)

This religious organisation claimed by the mid 1990s a worldwide membership of 4.9 million active Witnesses in 75,500 congregations in 232 countries (*The Watchtower* Jan. 1, 1995). Jehovah's Witnesses spend on average 10 hours a month evangelising from door to door, and 5 hours a week attending meetings. They are instructed to "avoid independent thinking" (*The Watchtower* Jan. 15, 1993) and devote 85 percent of their personal study time to *Watchtower* publications and 15 percent to their version of the Bible. The organisation is said to be growing at the rate of 4,000 converts a week and is building five Kingdom Halls a week worldwide! Their magazine *The Watchtower* is published twice a month in 120 languages, with each issue having an average printing of over 16 million copies, and over 600,000 are for distribution in the U.K. Their other major magazine is *Awake*.

Jehovah's Witnesses are a zealously committed religious group and yet they have no personal relationship with Jesus Christ and no assurance of salvation. "The key teaching of the Watchtower Society is that its governing body is God's only channel of communication on earth today." (Kern). Their leaders maintain that there is no salvation outside the Watchtower Society.

## History

The Jehovah's Witnesses were originally known as "Russellites" after the name of their founder and first president **Charles Taze Russell** (1852-1916). He was born in Pittsburgh, Pennsylvania, and in 1870 organised a Bible class. He founded "Zion's Watchtower" in 1879 and in 1886 he published the first volume of *The Millennial Dawn*. There are seven volumes in all, six written by Russell, these are now known as, *Studies in Scripture* and in effect are more highly valued by Jehovah's Witnesses than the Bible. The second president was **Judge Joseph Franklin Rutherford** (d. 1942), whose leadership gave the movement the title of "Jehovah's Witnesses" based on Isaiah 43.10. He established the headquarters in Brooklyn, New York and gave himself complete authority over the movement. **Nathan H. Knorr** was the third president (d. 1977). He was an able administrator who built up membership from 115,000 to over two million. During his leadership the Watchtower's own English 'translation' of the Bible known as *The New Translation of the Holy Scripture* was produced in 1961. The fourth president was **Frederick W. Franz** (d.1992). He was the spokesman for the translation committee, though he had no recognised qualifications in Hebrew or Greek. There now seems to be more of a collective leadership under the presidency of **Milton G. Henschel**.

## Characteristics

Jehovah's Witnesses meet regularly in local centres known as "Kingdom Halls" for study, reading, theocratic school and congregational activities. They are well known for their door to door evangelism, home Bible study groups, refusal to celebrate Christmas and birthdays or to allow blood transfusions for their members. Witnesses tend to be very sincere, hard working and good living people. In addition they are persistent to the point of tenacity in following up contacts. They are well trained to answer common objections and they also receive serious warnings to be aware of friends and relatives who may be "used by Satan" to try to dissuade them from adhering to Witness teaching. They are warned about "apostate" literature such as testimonies of former Witnesses and live in constant fear of being "disfellowshipped" because family and friends who remain as Witnesses will then shun them.

**Beliefs**

Jehovah's Witnesses claim to accept the Bible as their only authority, yet they deny the trinity, the deity and bodily resurrection of Christ, salvation by grace through faith and the eternal punishment of the wicked. They have a tendency to quote Biblical verses out of context, ignore other relevant passages altogether and are carefully and specifically trained to follow certain lines of thought through Scripture. They seem to be encouraged to read the Bible only under the strict supervision of their leaders through publications from headquarters. The following are some examples of their misuse of Scripture.

**John 14.28**

In this verse the Lord Jesus says, "My Father is greater than I". Jehovah's Witnesses use this to support their contention that the Lord Jesus was not God.

However, the verse has a clear reference to the voluntary subordination of the Lord Jesus to His Father's will. This was the human Jesus submitting Himself to His Father's will. This verse makes no comment upon His essential nature which is divine, only His temporary rank while here on earth. So the 'greater than' refers to His position on earth, rather than whom He is. Further reading in such passages as Hebrews 1.8; Isaiah 9.6; Mark 14.61-62; 1 John 2.22-23 and Philippians 2.6, clearly and powerfully emphasise the deity of Christ.

## Colossians 1.15

In this verse the Lord Jesus is called the "firstborn" of all creation. Jehovah's Witnesses claim that this means "first created" and implies that Jesus was not an eternal being and is someone less than the eternal God. Yet "firstborn" is used and not "first created" and the writer Paul, great intellectual that he was, would not have confused the issue by using "firstborn" if in fact he had meant "first created". The term "firstborn" does not refer to birth but to a pre-eminent position. The nation of Israel is referred to as "firstborn" (Exodus 4.22; Jeremiah 31.9) but was clearly not the first nation on earth. It was the nation most highly favoured by God. So "firstborn" refers to favoured rank, not position through birth.

## John 1.1

*The New Translation of the Holy Scriptures* includes the following statement in John 1.1, "the Word was a god" rather than "the Word was God". It is true that in this verse the Greek word for God "theos" is used twice, once with the definite article and once without. Jehovah's Witnesses use this to justify their use of "a god". Yet even in their own translation they are inconsistent, for in the first eighteen verses of John chapter 1, "theos" appears six times without the definite article in v.6, v.12, v.13, v.18 (twice) as well as in v.1. It is rendered as "God" in each instance except for the last clause of the first verse. To be consistent they should say, "a man sent from a god" (v.6) and "the sons of a god" (v.12), but such renderings would make a nonsense of the text. The term "a god" is only used in the first verse to undermine the truth of the deity of Christ. There are no reputable authorities or translations that support the rendering, "the Word was a god". It should be noted that the absence of the definite article does not indicate someone other than the true God. "Theos" is used "quite predominantly of the true God, sometimes with, sometimes without the article" *Greek-English Lexicon of the New Testament*; Arndt & Gingrech. The Jehovah's Witness use of "a god" indicates that their religion is polytheistic and believe in more than one god, for they say "the Word was with God and the Word was a god", clearly for them the Word is another god separate from the true God. The Bible knows only one God and His name is Jehovah. The Christian faith is monotheistic.

Jehovah's Witnesses refuse to believe in the deity and personality of the Holy Spirit. They refuse salvation as a gift of grace, believing that it can be achieved through such works as going from door to door selling and distributing literature. Most Jehovah's Witnesses believe that they will inherit eternal life on earth, while a select 144,000 will be privileged to go to Heaven. They deny the reality of Hell, making the work of Christ on the cross invalid. They believe that those who do not go to Heaven or inherit the earth are simply terminated and so will no longer exist.

Today they claim that the Lord returned in 1914, coming invisibly and setting up His kingdom in Heaven. Yet Russell and Watchtower teaching prophesied that the kingdom would be set up *on earth* in 1914! *(Watchtower Reprints* Vol.1, March 1880 p.82). They also prophesied that "the full establishment of the kingdom of God *in the earth* at A.D. 1914, the terminus of the Gentiles" (Russell in *Thy kingdom Come* 1891, p. 126). They changed this teaching when the prophecy was unfulfilled; therefore the Jehovah's Witness religion can justly be called a false cult.

## Encountering the Jehovah's Witnesses

When Christian believers encounter Jehovah's Witnesses we must not view them as enemies. Their teaching is false, but they believe it to be true and they hold that view with all sincerity. We must always be gracious, kind and listening and never aggressive or arrogant. Our aim must be to win them for Christ and so we need to be prepared and that will require study, reading and memorisation of Scripture. We need knowledge both of the Bible and where that differs from Jehovah's Witness teaching. We must learn that certain approaches will be counter productive. For example, to present a testimony of a converted "Witness" will not impress or shock but will raise suspicions and bring a rapid end to the conversation, because "Witnesses" are specifically warned about such books. It is worth trying to examine beliefs in the light of Scripture. Ask leading questions and gradually sow the seeds of doubt about Jehovah's Witness doctrine on the basis of what the Scriptures teach. Don't rush from proof text to proof text, examine each one within its context and honestly seek the correct meaning of the verse together. Be prayerful. Nothing will be achieved apart from the power of the Holy Spirit. He alone can take our words and the reading of the Bible and make them effective in the lives of those with whom we speak. The reality of Christian testimony can be very powerful. Take any opportunity to share experiences of the Lord and to show by life the reality of what it means to be a Christian.

Live with expectation that God will answer prayer. The Watchtower is not impregnable and it is encouraging to know that many Jehovah's Witnesses come to Christ each year. Often they testify that it was conversations with Christians that enabled them to see the Watchtower deception. Therefore every Christian has a valuable contribution to make in the evangelisation of Jehovah's Witnesses.

# The Church of Jesus Christ
# of Latter-Day Saints
# (Mormons)

The Mormon Church still has strong political influence in the state of Utah in the U.S.A.. It owns the second largest financial institution west of the Mississippi, The Beneficial Life Insurance Company, which has enormous land holdings, as well as a controlling interest in the Los Angeles Times. It is very missionary orientated and encourages its most promising young people to dedicate two years of their lives to missionary work on a self-supporting basis. These young people are always well dressed, polite and give a very wholesome image. This cult is unusual in that it does not try to keep its people in ignorance but actively encourages its members to gain university and college qualifications.

## History
**Joseph Smith Jr.** (b. 1805 in Sharon, Vermont, U.S.A.) founded the Mormon Church. In 1817 his parents moved the family to Rochester in New York State and there most of them joined the local Presbyterian Church. Smith was undecided about which denomination to join – an indecision that became the basis of his future church. He then claimed to receive a number of visions. The first was in 1820 when

he was told not to join any denomination, as they were all evil. In 1823 the angel Moroni informed him of buried golden plates and in 1827 he was granted permission to dig them up. He then claimed to have translated those plates, supposedly written in a reformed Egyptian language, and published the results in 1830. An angel then removed the plates! This unlikely episode is made even less credible by the fact that there were no reliable witnesses to verify the existence of such plates.

April 6th, 1830 marked the official opening of "the Church of Christ" at Fayette, New York, with an initial membership of six. Membership grew and many moved west to Kirtland, Ohio, where Smith supervised the first printing of his divine revelations. This book was originally entitled *Book of Commandments* but has since undergone many significant changes and is now called *Doctrines and Covenants*.

Following persecution Smith was imprisoned. He managed to escape and lead his followers to Nauvoo, Illinois, where he organised a small army and designated himself as Lieutenant General. His followers built a temple and attempted to gain new members for their church. However, Smith and his followers found themselves criticised in the pages of the local newspaper, *The Nauvoo Expositor* and they attacked and destroyed the presses and burnt copy. These actions led to the arrest and imprisonment of Smith and after a brief release, he was rearrested and jailed at Carthage, Illinois. He was killed when a mob stormed the prison on June 27th, 1844. Thus although the founder and prophet of the movement had died, his martyrdom ensured his revered place in Mormon history.

Smith's successor was **Brigham Young**, who became

president of the 'Twelve Apostles', with most followers accepting his leadership. To escape the continued persecution he led the great trek westward in 1847 to Salt Lake Valley. This was established as Mormon headquarters and occupies that position to this day. Young had a great influence on the development of Mormonism but was also a ruthless leader. He it was who ordered the 'Mountain Meadow Massacre' of 100 non-Mormons, an episode that is a severe embarrassment to modern Mormons. Membership had risen to 150,000 by 1877 when Young died and numbers have continued to grow and today the organisation claims well over five million adherents.

A rival organisation was founded and set up headquarters in Wisconsin in 1853. This minority has stayed loyal to the Smith family maintaining that Joseph Smith's son was the only true and rightful successor. This organisation is known as "The Reformed Church of Jesus Christ of Latter-Day Saints", and refuses to be termed "Mormon". With over 200,000 members it has not thrived like the parent church. However, it is an irritant to the Mormon Church.

## Claims

Mormons believe that they are the restoration of the true church established by Jesus Christ and that all other churches and denominations are both wrong and evil. They use four books as the basis of authority.

**The Bible**: To them the Bible is inspired but polluted. They maintain that certain passages have been added and others removed, especially by the Catholic Church. Thus they do not really trust the Bible and place much more faith in the other three books.

**The Book of Mormon**: They believe that God

inspired this book which is a purported history of two great civilisations in America. The original author of the book was supposedly the prophet Mormon.

**Doctrines and Covenants**: This gives 136 revelations outlining distinctive Mormon doctrines, including baptism for the dead and celestial marriage.

**The Pearl of Great Price**: This contains:

**a. The Book of Moses**: which is equivalent to the first six chapters of Genesis.

**b. The Book of Abraham**: which is a claimed translation from Egyptian papyrus and has been proved to be fraudulent.

**c. A History of Joseph Smith.**

**d. Articles of Faith.**

It is worth noting that the Mormon Scriptures contradict themselves as well as the Bible.

## Beliefs and Practices

Mormons do not believe in one God. They deny the deity of Christ and hence the Trinity. They deny the doctrine of hell and punishment and seem to believe that salvation is for everyone.

**God**: God is viewed in a number of ways.

**a. Polytheistic**: They accept many gods. "In the beginning the head of the Gods called a council of the Gods" (Joseph Smith)

**b. An Exalted Man**: They accept that God was once a man. "God was once as we are now, and is an exalted man." (Joseph Smith)

**c. Physical**: "The Father has a body of flesh and bone as tangible as man's" (Joseph Smith)

**Jesus Christ**: They claim that Jesus is not the unique Son of God, only being different from other men because he became the firstborn of God's 'spirit children'.

**Man**: They believe that man is a pre-existent soul who takes his body at birth.

**Salvation**: They claim that everyone goes to one of three levels of glory:

**a. The Celestial Kingdom**: This is the highest of the three heavens in Mormon teaching and is reserved for the Melchizedek priesthood which consists of members who will become gods.

**b. The Terrestrial Kingdom**: This is reserved for those who failed the requirements of exaltation to the Celestial Kingdom.

**c. The Telestial Kingdom**: This is reserved for those who have no belief in Christ or the Gospel.

**Polygamy**: This is the belief in the doctrine of plural marriages, namely that a man may have many wives. This belief and practice led to some of the early persecution of Mormonism. Brigham Young's polygamy is recounted in a book by his twenty-seventh wife.

**Racism**: Mormons relegate Black people and Indians into a class of their own. Such people cannot become priests and very little work is done among them to draw them in as members of the church. Thus very real discrimination has been practised against black people. In the *Pearl of Great Price* Joseph Smith wrote: "For behold the Lord shall curse the land with much heat, and the barrenness thereof shall go forth forever; and there was a blackness come upon all the children of Canaan, that they were despised...for the seed of Cain were black, and had not place among them". Thus historically Mormonism has not looked favourably upon Black people. In the present climate of civil rights and anti-racialism it seems that this policy has at least been officially changed.

## Note on the Book of Mormon

This book gives a very definite account of the origin of the American Indians and how they came to live in the Western Hemisphere. It was supposedly translated from a reformed Egyptian language and is very much revered by present day Mormons. Yet it has been scrutinised by academics and been severely critiqued. "The book is untrue Biblically, historically and scientifically." (William Duncan Strong, Columbia University). Essentially there is no evidence archaeological, linguistic or historical to support the accounts contained in the Book of Mormon. No names, cities, persons, nations or places mentioned in the book have ever been found or identified. Also no genuine Egyptian inscriptions have ever been found in America and nothing has been remotely similar to Smith's reformed Egyptian. There is no such language.

## False Prophecy

Joseph Smith claimed that the Lord told him that the "Saints" would build a temple in Zion, Jackson County, Missouri, during his generation, and that Zion would never be removed from its place. "This generation shall not all pass away until an house shall be built unto the Lord...upon the consecrated spot as I have appointed." (*Doctrine and Covenants*)  Again he wrote: "Surely Zion is the city of our God, and surely Zion cannot fall, neither be moved out of place, for God is there, and the hand of the Lord is there..." (*Doctrine and Covenants*).  These prophecies failed since a temple was never built at the appointed place. Moreover, two weeks before Smith gave the prophecy that Zion would not be "moved out of her place" the Mormons were unceremoniously run out of Zion, their printing presses were destroyed and some of their leaders were tarred and feathered. Smith was in Kirtland, Ohio at the time and so was uninformed of the situation in Jackson County when he gave his prophetic statement.

The Bible says that, "When a prophet speaks in the name of the LORD, if the thing follow not, nor come to pass, that is the thing which the LORD has not spoken, but the prophet has spoken it presumptuously: thou shall not be afraid of him." (Deuteronomy 18.22). Clearly in the light of such a strong Biblical statement Joseph Smith must be classified as a false prophet and therefore the Mormon faith is founded on falsehood and must be described clearly as a false religion.

# The Holy Spirit Association for the Unification of World Christianity

Members of this religious movement are commonly called "Moonies" after the founder the Rev. Sung Myung Moon. This movement has emerged as one of the larger cults to be established in the twentieth century. It is said to have over two million members world-wide and to have a business empire worth billions of dollars. It owns *The Washington Times* which is one of the newspapers that has been used for White House daily news summaries. This movement has attracted much media attention for the following reasons:

1. A large number of adherents have in the past engaged in street selling of items such as plastic flowers and badges, as well as seeking donations for the various social activities in which the movement is said to be involved.

2. The practice of mass weddings in which hundreds of couples had their marriage ceremonies conducted simultaneously by the Rev. Moon.

3. The imprisonment of the Rev. Moon in Danbury's federal penitentiary for tax evasion, where he served a thirteen-month sentence.

4. There have been various charges of brainwashing by this organisation and there have been some attempts by parent groups to kidnap and deprogramme children caught up in the movement.

The whole movement has been described as "a mind boggling mixture of Pentecostal Christianity, Eastern mysticism, anti-communism, pop psychology and metaphysics."

## History

The history of the Unification Church centres around the Rev. Sung Myung Moon, a Korean, born on the 6th January 1920. He belonged to a family that converted to Presbyterian Christianity in 1931. In his mid teens Moon claimed to experience a vision of Jesus Christ who commissioned him to build up God's kingdom on earth. God is said to have given him new insights into the teaching of the Bible and to have enabled him to reinterpret the Scriptures.

He has apparently been married four times and may not have legally ended the second marriage. He has supposedly dabbled in the occult, and been arrested and tortured by the communist North Korean regime. He was linked with the Korean Central Intelligence Agency and a Japanese organised crime syndicate and has been imprisoned for sex offences.

In 1951 he founded his church in Seoul, South Korea, and eventually set up headquarters in the United States in 1971. In 1957 he published *Divine Principle* a book of over 500 pages which is said to be the fulfilment of John 16.13 where the Lord Jesus talks about the Spirit of truth who "will show you things to come". Moonies effectively use *Divine Principle* as their guiding light considering it much more important than the Bible. They view history as divided into three ages: the Old Testament age which used the Old Testament; the New Testament age that used the New Testament and the Completed New Testament age that uses Divine Principle.

Moon declared that Jesus, the second Adam failed in his mission and so a third Adam was needed, known as the Messiah, the Lord of the Second Advent. Though he did not claim publicly to be that Messiah, it was always implied from his writing and teaching that he was so. In 1992 he finally declared publicly that he was the Messiah. "Amidst the splendour of the magnificent Little Angels Performing Arts Centre in Seoul, Rev. Sun Myung Moon announced in this speech on August 24, 1992, to a distinguished audience of current and former heads of state, scholars, professors and religious leaders, that he and Mrs Moon were the Lord of the Second Coming – the True Parents - the Messiah." (*Unification Newsletter*. Vol.8, No. 1, Jan.1993, p.2)

There are many front organisations behind which the Unification Church operates, some of which are seemingly innocuous, but can draw the unwary into this religious movement. Members are willing to lie and deceive to make sales or gain donations. They view telling lies as acceptable because money is being taken from people under Satan's control to be used in God's work. Members often have a daily quota of income to meet. They have been known to infiltrate churches and Christian Unions to encourage the disaffected and those with problems to defect and join the Unification Church.

## Teaching

Foundational to the Rev. Moon's teaching is the concept of dualism, which is similar to the Chinese "yin and yang" belief of Taoism. This belief views the whole of existence as duality. So human life is male and female. There is positive and negative, protons and electrons and so on. By working this principle backwards they view God in terms of both mother and father. A brief exploration of some of their teachings clearly show them to be at variance with Scripture.

## The Fall of Man into Sin

The account in Genesis is very clear and reveals disobedience to the direct command of God, through the temptation brought by Satan to eat fruit from the forbidden tree. However, *Divine Principle* claims to be the first 'correct' interpretation of this event. The Rev. Moon insists that there were two falls. The first was physical and the second was spiritual and both he apparently claims were sexual in nature. Physically Eve's fall was her sexual relationship with Adam and that occurred after her spiritual fall which was the result of sexual relations with Lucifer. As well as an expression of breathtaking arrogance this reveals a fixation with sexual activity on the part of the Rev. Moon, who has had charges of sexual perversion against him and has apparently been married four times.

## Salvation

In Moon's teaching there has to be a dual aspect to man's salvation, both physical and spiritual. He claims that Christ on the Cross accomplished spiritual salvation, while he, Moon, the 'third Adam' will accomplish physical salvation by setting up the perfect family. So he views the work of Christ as only partly successful and states, "The cross cannot completely liquidate our original sin" (*Divine Principle* p.142)

## Jesus Christ

The Rev. Moon denies the deity of Jesus Christ, insisting that He is not God and states "he can by no means be God Himself". He even goes as far as to say that followers of the Unification Church can supersede Jesus. In his own words he states, "You can compare yourself with Jesus Christ, and feel you can be greater than Jesus Himself." He generally views Jesus as a failure as for example when he states, "Abraham was the father of faith, Moses was the man of faith, Jesus was the son of man, trying to carry out his mission at the cost of his own life. But they are in a way failures." Again we witness the arrogance of Rev. Moon and his lack of understanding of New Testament truth.

The teaching of *Divine Principle* is at odds with the Bible in all its central points. It therefore cannot be considered in any way as the completion of God's revelation. The Rev. Moon has no messianic credentials and must be considered a false prophet. The Lord Jesus warned us of such people when he said, "Beware of false prophets who come to you in sheep's clothing but inwardly are ravenous wolves. You will know them by their fruits." (Matthew 7.15-16).

## Gospel Presentation

Christians need to show deep care and love to those who are caught up in this intensive and life dominating religion. It will be difficult to gain a hearing with members of the Unification Church because right from the outset they will be deeply suspicious and even concerned about possible persecution. This is because the Rev. Moon warns his followers that, "Christians of today will be the first to persecute the Messiah at the time of the Second Advent" (*Divine Principle* p.533).

A great deal of gentle patience will have to be exercised as many Moonies are disturbed souls who have been brainwashed and kept so busy that they hardly have time to think and certainly have no energy to question what they do and what they believe. We need to formulate questions that get them thinking about the veracity of some of the teaching and practices of the Rev. Moon. Questions must be formulated in a genuine desire to seek information and not with a sense aggression or interrogation.

They have to be encouraged to read various passages of the Bible, especially those that deal with God's love and Christ's work on the cross. They do not accept the Bible as the final revelation from God, but they do use it to find facts to support their theology. Christians need to bathe their witness in prayer and seek the Lord's wisdom and love to lead these precious and sincere souls to saving faith in Jesus Christ.

# The Church of Christ Scientist

This religious movement is known as "Christian Science" and has drawn the scathingly critical description of "being neither Christian nor scientific" (Harold J. Berry). Their centres of activity are called "reading rooms" and in more recent days there has been a greater interest in their written works as the result of the increasing influence of metaphysics. Western society has now a greater focus upon the mysterious, the spiritual and new age alternative healing. This has enabled Christian Science to find an increasing readership and to have a greater impact than ever before.

**History**

**Mary Baker Eddy** (1821-1910) founded the movement in New England in the United States. She was born into a devoutly religious family and joined the Congregational Church at the age of seventeen, even though she claimed not to accept the full theology of that church. She was married three times, firstly to George Glover. The marriage although happy lasted only just over half a year when Glover died leaving her with an unborn child. Her second marriage to Daniel Patterson ended in divorce on the grounds of his desertion, though she later claimed that he was an adulterer. The third husband was Asa Gilbert Eddy who had been one of her students and was the first to assume the title of "Christian Science Practitioner".

Mary Baker was a sickly child, suffering with spinal weakness, seizures and nervous collapse. After the birth of her son she was never again totally free from pain and she was further painfully injured when she fell on an icy pavement on February 1st 1866. It is therefore of little surprise that she had a fixation with health and healing, and the need for deliverance from pain. That fall on the pavement was, she later claimed, the turning point in her life. Her recollection of the event was that her injuries were pronounced fatal by the doctors, but through reading the account of the healing of the paralysed man in Matthew 9.2-8 she heard the voice of God telling her to get up. This she did and thereafter enjoyed better health than ever before. From then on she was determined to devote her life to the healing element of religion. She carried on a healing practice, taught others her healing principles and set her ideas down in writing.

In 1879, "The Church of Christ Scientist" was incorporated, with headquarters in Boston. There were many problems, court cases to attend and internal tensions to be defused and increasingly she found herself under pressure. Ill health once again overtook her and despite her teaching she did consult medical practitioners for the relief of pain and justified these "non-mental measures" as best she could. When her husband, Asa, died she claimed that he had been murdered with "arsenic mentally administered"! And when she viewed her own demise she urged one of her close associates to say that if she died she had been "mentally murdered".

Her ideas are the essential framework for belief in the Christian Science Church and are found in her books, *Science and Health* (1875) and *Key to the Scriptures* (1883). These were subsequently revised and eventually standardised in 1907. The movement is now organised by a self-perpetuating board of directors, the first members of whom were appointed by Mrs Eddy, and they apparently use her book *Church Manual* (1895) as the basic foundation for governing the church. The manual contains all the rules for organising the church and no rules could be changed without the authorisation of the leader. Thus Mrs Eddy had absolute control in her own lifetime and subsequently the organisation has proved to be highly authoritarian.

It is estimated that there are over three million adherents worldwide, though this is an educated guess as one of Mrs Eddy's rules was that numbers of members were not to be published. Their newspaper *The Christian Science Monitor* is highly respected and is not simply a channel for the religious views of the Christian Science Church but an important vehicle for the distribution of world news. They publish other journals in over twelve languages and also have regular media programmes.

## Claims

They claim that the Bible is their final authority. However *Science and Health* is seen as new and exclusive divine truth and in practice this publication supersedes the Bible in the eyes of Christian Scientists, especially as they believe the Bible contains errors. It would seem that in reality much of the beliefs and practices of Christian Science was plagiarised from a nineteenth century mesmerist Phineas P. Quimby. His work was clearly well known to Mary Baker Eddy, but also there is considerable evidence that she used the writings of others and incorporated them into her work pretending that they were original to her.

Christian Scientists meet for 'services' but no sermons are given. There are readings from *Science and Health* and from the Bible and the same readings are followed by all Christian Science churches worldwide. Hymns may be sung, as well as solos, there are periods of silent prayer and the Lord's prayer will be repeated.

## Beliefs

Essentially their theology is a revived form of the first century Gnostic heresy that stated that material substance is inherently evil, while the non-material is good. So there can be no coexistence between the spirit and the body. Such teaching can be summarised as, "Mind is all, Matter is nought". Such a view by its very nature must deny the incarnation of Christ and His essential deity. They would argue that the true spiritual essence of God could not inhabit a corrupt physical body.

The personal God of the Bible is denied and for Christian Science believers God is inseparable from the creation. This pantheistic idea is essentially an eastern religious concept and runs counter to historical Christian belief. They have no concept of heaven and hell, do not believe in final judgement or the resurrection of the body. Also they find personal prayer a logical impossibility, as they believe God to be a principle rather than a person. They view sin as an illusion and therefore Christ's atoning sacrifice on the cross is unnecessary. To be 'saved' according to Christian Science belief requires faith in Christ's work as interpreted by Mrs Eddy together with one's own work. They do not practice baptism, or the Lord's

Supper and have no belief in the Second Coming of Christ.

They make great claims for healing power but most claims are utterly unverifiable. It often appears to be psychosomatic rather than organic healing that takes place. Yet Christian Science has tapped into a productive vein of thought in the human mind as people increasing desire to be fit and healthy.

## Terminology

Some of the terminology used by Christian Scientists include:

**Animal Magnetism:** This is believed to be wrong thinking and can cause individuals to experience the illusion of evil. Malicious animal magnetism can kill those it is practised against.

**At-one-ment:** In Christian Science theology this appears to be the unity formed between the 'mind' of God and that of man as demonstrated by Christ.

**Immortal Mind:** This is the term for 'God' in Christian Science theology.

**Mortal Mind:** This is the source of the illusion of evil, sickness, sin and death in Christian Science belief.

## Conclusion

Both disease and death are denied in Christian Science teaching. Mrs Eddy taught that disease was a mental, mortal fear, a mistaken belief, an illusion and a delusion. She claimed that "Man is never sick, for mind is not sick and matter cannot be". Thus for Christian Science the cure of sickness is to help the person understand that he is not really sick, that his pain is imaginary and that his imagined disease is only the result of a false belief!

Mrs Eddy also denied the reality of death by claiming

43

that "Any material evidence of death is false, for it contradicts the spiritual facts of being". Indeed she never provided an official ritual for funerals, though she provided orders of services for other occasions. Her own death was something of an embarrassment to the church, as it would seem that she herself had insufficient faith to avoid the experience of dying.

Clearly the theology of Christian Science is a mish mash of ideas gleaned by Mrs Eddy. Her teaching, without question, has done untold harm to families and individuals who have been denied the essential help of the medical profession and have therefore endured pain, discomfort, immobility and even the prospect of premature death. To allow such suffering and also to deny the central truths of the Christian faith places Christian Science very firmly in the category we call false cults. "Christian Scientists, therefore, have no more right to apply to themselves the title *Christian* than have Buddhists or Hindus – with whose teachings, indeed, Christian Science has greater affinity than with those of Christianity." (Hoekema)

# Unitarianism

In 1959 the Unitarian Universalist Church was founded by the amalgamation of the Unitarians and Universalists. This church is largely found in the United States, has a membership of less than 250,000 but has a worldwide influence. Its teaching has been described as "the doctrine of reason" (Berry) because the emphasis is not upon God's revelation of truth, but upon man's ability to formulate truth. Unitarianism teaches that there is one solitary entity known as God, who has revealed himself through various men and numerous religious writings. None of these are infallible and all contribute to the religious growth and development of mankind. Thus they view God as a "Uni-personality" and deny the doctrine of the Trinity, namely "one God, eternally existent in three persons".

## History

Unitarianism is really the modern manifestation of an ancient heresy known as Arianism. This doctrine denied the full deity of Christ and was condemned by the early church fathers and rejected as part of the early church creeds. It was given little credence and had few followers until the sixteenth century when it spread throughout various parts of Europe. The main articulator of this view was an Italian named **Fausto Sozini** who is better known in history as **Socinus** (1539 –1604). He built upon the work of his uncle Lelio and others to develop anti-Trinitarian doctrines. Thus he denied the Trinity and especially the deity of Christ and that is the Unitarian position to this day.

His views became deeply rooted in Poland, Hungary and Transylvania, eventually spreading to Holland, Britain and the United States. The modern movement truly flourished in America partly as a reaction to the rigid Calvinism of Puritanism in New England. Many who espoused Unitarianism were prominent in literary, political and religious circles. **Jonathan Mayhew** (1720-1766) was minister of the West Church in Boston and that church is considered the first Unitarian Church in New England. **William Ellery Channing** (1780-1842) has been dubbed the "Apostle of Unitarianism". **Ralph Waldo Emerson** and **Joseph Priestley** also espoused Unitarianism.

The American Unitarian Association was formed in 1825, while in 1865 the National Unitarian Conference was organised. Through this period a theology was being developed and various ideas were being formulated. This all culminated in the International Congress of Unitarianism held in 1900. Here Unitarian views and doctrines were confirmed and these have hardly been revised in the last hundred years. This teaching accepts evolution, empirical methods of religion, higher criticism and ethical attempts to try and realize the higher affirmations of Christianity.

The growth of Unitarianism resulted in a major cleavage in the Congregational Church of America and led to Harvard College being lost to the evangelical cause. The emphasis of Unitarianism upon education and practical philanthropy was much more acceptable to cultural and influential people than the evangelical emphasis upon home and foreign mission work to win the lost for Christ.

## Beliefs

**The Bible:** They do not accept that the Bible is the inspired, infallible Word of God. Though historic Christianity has always believed that the Old and New Testaments are fully inspired by God and are therefore without error, Unitarians claim that Protestants in the seventeenth century manufactured the doctrine of an infallible Bible to combat the teaching of Roman Catholicism. They view the Bible as a creation of man and believe that it is replete with inaccuracies, inconsistencies and errors. They deny its authority and believe that human reason is the highest authority. They will quote from the Bible whenever it supports their ideas, but so often quote out of context. Also they are reluctant to reject the Bible totally as it does enable them to appear as orthodox Christian believers, which may give them acceptance in certain circles.

**Jesus Christ:** Unitarianism demotes the Lord Jesus from deity, namely His position as God the Son, to the level of simply a good man. "Unitarians repudiate the doctrine and dogma of the Virgin Birth...Unitarians do not believe that Jesus is the Messiah, either of Jewish hope or of Christian fantasy. They do not believe He is 'God Incarnate', or the Second Person of the Trinity, as the final arbitrator at the end of time, who shall come to judge the quick and the dead." (Rev. Carl M. Chorowsky, Unitarian minister) Thus they believe that orthodox Christianity has forsaken the true human Jesus and has distorted His memory by shrouding it with claims of being deity and Saviour of the world. They believe Jesus to have been an exceptional man who, as a teacher, made a contribution to the religious advancement of the human race.

**Salvation:** They deny that salvation is through Christ alone and instead, "Unitarians speak warmly of

47

salvation...in terms of character. We prefer to think of it as an achievement dependent on deeds rather than creeds." (Jack Mendelsohn, Unitarian writer). Thus they believe in "self salvation", but it is not a salvation from the judgement and torment of hell, because they refuse to accept the reality of hell. They do not believe that a loving God would ever send anyone to such a place and as 'Universalists' they accept that everyone will one day be in a right relationship with God. They actually feel repelled at the very notion of the total depravity of man and certainly of the idea that a loving God would sacrifice His Son on the cross for the sins of the world. Thus they reject God's way of salvation and prefer to formulate their own. So they do not believe in the work of mission and do not send out any missionaries. "By deliberate choice we send no missionaries over the face of the earth to convert others to our way of believing...We generally feel that people of other religions have as much to teach us as we have to teach them" (Mendelsohn).

**Theology**: Unitarianism is extreme liberal theology, otherwise known as "modernism" or "theology of the school of higher criticism". This denies the verbal inspiration of Scripture and requires its adherents to make allowance for the imperfections and errors found in the Bible. Therefore the only authoritative statements are those made by 'wise' scholars of modernism. Human reason is exalted and Biblical authority denied. It is said of Dr Mayhew, "He unhesitatingly applied the rational method to all theological problems, and to him reason was the final court of appeal for everything connected with religion." (Berry)

Not all Unitarians are found in Unitarian churches. It would seem that many are found in churches where

Trinitarian truth is taught. "It appears to be a matter of policy for a fifth-column of ministers with Unitarian leanings to infiltrate the churches, with a view to future conquest". (Saunders). One former Unitarian minister has written, "although the Unitarians as a denomination are very weak, the spirit of Unitarianism is very prevalent. There are thousands of churches that would resent being classed in such company, but in reality they belong nowhere else. Their evangelism is nothing more than an appeal to the will and their gospel is a setting forth of the manhood of Christ. If it were not for the left-over fire of a former generation they would be as fruitless as the Unitarian denomination itself."

It is impossible to give this religion the title of "Christian" because it denies all the essential elements of historic Christianity. Indeed some even of their own leaders are reluctant to take the title "Christian" and have publicly announced that they are not altogether sure whether they can classify themselves as Christians. "I am willing to call myself a Christian only if in the next breath I am permitted to say in varying degrees I am also a Jew, a Hindu, a Moslem, a Buddhist, a Stoic, and an admirer of Akhenaten, Zoroaster, Confucius, Lao-tse and Socrates" (Jack Mendelsohn in *Why I Am a Unitarian*).

"Unitarianism is characterised not so much by its beliefs as its 'unbeliefs'." (Saunders). It denies the Bible as the Word of God, the deity of Christ, the Trinity, the Virgin Birth, the bodily resurrection of Christ and His Second Coming. Unitarians deny the reality of hell and the judgement of God. They deny the sinfulness of man, viewing people as basically good and steadily improving as a race. Unitarianism is a mishmash of human ideas and the theology can change at the dictates of human reason, so-called new evidence and the latest ideas from science, philosophy and creative thinking.

The essential need for Unitarians is to realise that the Bible is God's Word and can be implicitly trusted. The Bible clearly teaches the deity of Christ and that salvation is only by grace through faith in the Lord Jesus, who died for our sins on the cross. Salvation means eternal life and the joyful anticipation of heaven, while rejection of Christ leads to eternal condemnation and removal from the presence of God.

# Christadelphianism

Nearly thirty years ago while in University I encountered my first Christadelphian. He was a student in the same hall of residence as myself. Together we talked about the Bible and started to consider spiritual truth in the light of the Scriptures. He believed sincerely that the Bible was the truth of God and it was a God-given blessing to see him growing into a fuller understanding of the true Gospel of Jesus Christ. The day came when he received Christ as his Lord and Saviour and entered into the wonderful experience of salvation. He eventually married a Christian girl and went overseas to serve the Lord in a Christian school. Trusting the Lord Jesus as Saviour was not easy for him as his family members were all Christadelphians and he was a third generation follower of Christadelphian teaching. However, the reality of Christ's presence enabled him to break with their false doctrine and be fully committed to the truth of the Gospel.

## History

The word "Christadelphian" is made up of two Greek words and means "Christ's brother" and as the name implies Christadelphians regard themselves as brethren of Christ. The movement was known as "Thomasism" in its early days, named after the founder **Dr. John Thomas** (1805-1871). Thomas was British but lived his life in America. However, he propounded his views both orally and in writing during three extended visits to Britain. Thus this religious movement is largely found in the United Kingdom.

Christadelphianism is one of the smallest of the religious cults in Britain and it was Thomas's successor Robert Roberts, baptised by Thomas in 1853 at the age of 14, who built upon the founder's views and established the central organisation in Birmingham in the English Midlands. This is not so much an official headquarters as a guiding light for local congregations each of which is considered independent and autonomous. The movement has less than 20,000 members in the United Kingdom, spread amongst 278 local congregations (*Religious Trends* 1998/1999). Writers on new religious movements tend to by-pass Christadelphianism because it is quite a small organisation which does not make headline news and also it is hardly found in the United States where most writing on religious cults emanates from.

Christadelphians meet in their own halls and refer to a local congregation as an "ecclesia". The word "ecclesia" is simply the Greek word for church. They have a commitment to and believe in studying the Authorised Version of the Bible and have preaching services with named subjects each week, with particular emphasis upon prophetic topics.

## Publications

Thomas published his ideas in *Elpis Israel* a title that means *The Hope of Israel.* It is subtitled "An Exposition of the Kingdom of God, with reference to the Time of the End and the Age to Come". This publication reveals that Thomas put his own ideas into interpretations of Scripture and stressed the importance of prophecy. The work is still revered by Christadelphians and a copy is presented to members at their baptism. Roberts also wrote an important book entitled, *Christendom Astray from the Bible* and this is still considered "one of Christadelphians most effective preaching aids". In 1844 Thomas started a monthly magazine *The Herald of the Future Age* but this is now known as the *The Christadelphian* and regarded as the official mouthpiece of the organisation.

## Beliefs

Christadelphians view **salvation** as possible through an understanding of the Bible, Christadelphian baptism and through the keeping of the commandments. Christadelphians cannot have any assurance of salvation and do not see the necessity to trust in the atoning work of Christ on the cross.

They deny the trinity and view **God** very much in physical rather than spiritual terms, as Roberts wrote, "..the Father is a tangible person". They deny the deity of **Jesus Christ**, state that he had no existence before his birth in Bethlehem and that he was not given the title of Christ until his baptism. The atoning work of Christ on the cross is of no importance to them.

Christadelphians do not accept the deity of the **Holy Spirit** and also deny his personality. They even claim that the Spirit is not at work in this present age, "there is no manifestation of the Spirit in these days" (Roberts).

They deny the existence of the **Devil**, believing that the names given to the Evil One in Scripture are simply manifestations within man himself. Heaven is regarded as the exclusive abode of God and that mankind "has no access into God's presence in heaven". Indeed they believe that "Heaven is not for man: his habitation, both now and in any future existence, is earth". They believe that all the faithful will be raised and given immortality when Christ reigns in His kingdom on earth. There is no **eternal future punishment** of the wicked, but annihilation of the unfaithful ones.

Christadelphians insist upon marriage within their own system and to break that rule or any of the other rules can lead to "disfellowshipping". To be "disfellowshipped" and put out of the church leads to the loss of any hope of eternal future blessing. Christadelphians must not serve in the armed forces or the police force and must not join political parties. In all they have a list of 35 doctrines to be rejected and a list of 53 commandments to be followed if they are to have any thought of future hope. Christadelphianism is very much a religion of works rather than of faith. The system offers the prospect of eternal blessing, but with no assurance that it can ever be achieved.

**Sharing our Faith**

Many Christadelphians have a profound understanding of Scripture and it is true that many have found a living faith in Christ through reading and studying the Bible for themselves, while still in Christadelphianism. This is encouraging because the Word of God is essential in any form of witnessing. Thus when we seek to share our faith we must not try to air knowledge as we might find that they know more than we do. However, we must with patience and love listen, explain and read the Bible in context, especially in the areas where Christadelphians deviate from the historical Christian faith. We need to support our witness with effective words of personal testimony by showing the wonderful effect of the Gospel upon our own lives. Such personal testimony is a very powerful weapon in leading Christadelphians to the Lord. Thus we must live consistent Christian lives and support all we say with committed prayer to the Lord to make our witness effective for His glory. "Remember we are not trying to win arguments, we might lose against superior head knowledge of Scripture. But we are presenting the reality of Jesus Christ in both what He has accomplished and what He means in our lives. This is what the Christadelphian needs." (Harris)

# The Central London
# Church of Christ

Towards the end of the 1980s I was at Aston University in Central Birmingham to speak at the Christian Union. Before I spoke a member of the University chaplaincy team gave details of and a brief warning about the cult known as the "Central London Church of Christ" (CLCOC). This cult had been banned from the campuses of King's College, London, the London School of Economics, Birmingham, Aston and Manchester Universities. As early as 1986 the "Universities and Colleges Christian Fellowship of Evangelical Unions" (UCCF) issued a statement disassociating itself from the CLCOC. The cult monitoring group "Family Action Information and Rescue" (FAIR) found that over a recent 12 month period the third most mentioned group amongst its calls for help was the "Central London Church of Christ". The only two groups with more calls for help were Scientology and the Unification Church (Moonies). The CLCOC has been described as "the fastest growing cult in Britain today", though this might have changed recently as it has expelled 400 of its members supposedly attempting to aid spiritual cleansing.

**History and Background**
The CLCOC has no connection with long established

churches of the same name. There are traditional Baptist-inspired Churches of Christ, which have nothing to do with this group. This cult has arisen in America largely due to the work and influence of **Kip Mckean**. He was converted at "The Crossroads Church of Christ" in Florida, USA. There he came under the influence of Charles "Chuck" Lucas who developed the technique of guiding converts, which became known as "discipling".

Mckean and his wife Elena moved to Boston in 1979 and set up the "Boston Church of Christ" using the techniques of discipling. The growth rate in Boston was staggering with as many as a thousand converts being baptized each year. In 1982 teams were sent to London and Chicago and from these other centres have been evangelized. The evangelists sent to London in 1982 were Douglas Arthur and James Lloyd. The former was given responsibility for the "Commonwealth Ministries", which included Britain, Australia, Hong Kong and India. Fred Scott, a young English concert pianist, became leader of the "London Church of Christ". There are now over 70 different centres worldwide, with plans for more to come.

## The organization

The CLCOC is a hierarchical organization with a very strong leadership principle. Obedience to the leadership is all-important and questioning is strictly discouraged. Independent thought is not easily tolerated. The essential structure is one of "discipling". Each recruit is put under the one-to-one supervision of a discipler, who is an established member of the congregation. Everyone has a discipler: new recruits are discipled by ordinary members, ordinary members are discipled by Bible study leaders, they are discipled by elders; elders by evangelists and so on up to the top small group who are discipled by Kip Mckean. The structure is very similar to a pyramid-selling operation.

The structure itself is not the problem, but the way in which it works produces disquiet. There has to be immediate obedience to the discipler who makes decisions about nearly every aspect of the life of the one being discipled. Leaders cannot be questioned, their word is final and this leads to a strong authoritarian system with the discipled being unable to think or make responsible decisions for themselves. This is what has caused deepest concern as Ian Howarth of Cult Information Centre says: "The Central Church of Christ is a sinister and dangerous cult which can affect people psychologically, spiritually, financially and even physically. It uses brainwashing and mind-control techniques. If I was in a position of influence with any university infiltrated by these people, I would do everything in my power to safeguard the welfare of students. They are at considerable risk."

## Beliefs and Teaching

In many ways the movement appears to hold traditional Protestant teaching. Their teaching about Jesus, the Trinity and the authority of the Bible appears to be correct. They resent the designation of "cult", "We are not a cult. We are a Christian church, which is attracting young people, because we are a lively exciting group. There is nothing sinister or underhand about us." (Tim Dannatt, leader of Birmingham Church of Christ). There is no doubt that Mckean's original motivation was altruistic and evangelistic and that he believed that he was helping those who followed him to find Christ. The leaders of this cult are very sincere people, and their teaching is very close to that of evangelical Christianity and in many ways sounds like the true faith. This makes their teaching difficult to distinguish from the truth of Scripture. There is no better counterfeit than that which is very close to the true currency.

The main features of CLCOC are:

**Exclusiveness:** Mckean and his followers now believe that they are the only true Christians in the world. This is a very powerful lever against any members who show signs of wavering.

**Salvation:** "We do not teach that salvation comes by faith alone...it should be noted that 'salvation by faith' is in no way identical with 'salvation by faith alone'." (Douglas Arthur) Essentially they teach that salvation is by faith and works which includes their baptism. This salvation they believe can be lost if followers do not persevere. They emphasize what people do, rather than what God has done, believing that they gain acceptance with God by their own efforts. So they teach that it is not so much what Christ has completed for us on the cross but what we do, ourselves, which brings about salvation.

**Baptism:** They teach that baptism is the moment of conversion, and has to be understood and practiced correctly for it to effective.

**Assurance:** Since salvation is not through faith alone, but involves works, assurance is only possible by having one's commitment checked by the church. This makes the members try hard, but leaves them guilt-ridden and without hope when they fail. This is of particular concern for the 400 who have been told that they have failed and have lost their salvation. Such people need particular care from concerned Christians.

**Authority:** The CLCOC claims that the Bible is their only authority, but in practice the teaching of the leaders has replaced the authority of the Bible. No one is allowed to question the teaching, independent thought is prevented and all responsibility for thinking is handed over to the leaders.

**Leadership:** The leaders require almost total obedience. However the Bible portrays leadership as servanthood, but CLCOC leaders are tyrannical, demanding obedience and determining the lives of the members.

**Pressure:** The leaders maintain discipline by keeping the members busy, so busy that the church totally dominates their lives and they have no time to think. Groups are manipulated to pressure people to conform by publicly praising or rebuking. For those who live in houses owned by the church, sleep deprivation and frequent fasting maintain the pressure to fully conform.

**Guilt:** If questioned the leaders usually answer in such a way as to induce guilt. They usually refuse to answer or suggest that the questioners by virtue of asking questions have something wrong with them, such as: being too proud, having a bad attitude or failing to make real progress. An ex-member writes: "Whenever I questioned these things, the following responses were most commonly given: 'That's not the issue - the issue is that you're not broken', 'It's in the Bible', 'I'm disappointed in you, how could you be questioning now?' or 'Brother, you just need to change'."

**Control:** The intensity of the relationship between discipler and discipled helps to control the members. Each one is encouraged to report all areas of life, confess sins and uncritically accept advice. Male-female relationships are rigidly controlled, with rules concerning the frequency of seeing each other and chaperoning.

**Deceit**: This cult has been known to use deceit to gain entry and acceptance. It has masqueraded in various forms. At the LSE it was called: "The Historical Literature Society", then "The Biblical Literature Society", while its congregation in North London was called "North London Christian Fellowship".

**Money**: Members are asked to donate 10% of their income and are constantly exhorted to contribute generously to other special appeals.

**Youth**: Members and leaders are mainly young people, usually recruited from higher education establishments. Many of these, who potentially were career and academic high-fliers, have had their future blighted by involvement with CLCOC. Some have dropped out of university studies, or ended up with poorer qualifications than expected.

## Why Do People Join?

Steve Wookey in his book *As Angels of Light* suggests four reasons:

1. The appeal of commitment is very great when compared with the apathy and general indifference of many churches.

2. Many become involved when they are away from home for the first time and are vulnerable to the friendship and concerned interest from members of the sect. This may particularly apply to overseas students.

3. Those who are uncertain about what they really believe may be attracted to the cult with its certainties and firm answers from leaders.

4. There are many genuine Christians who are sucked into this cult because they have never been fully taught in the Word of God.

In view of these reasons it will come as no surprise

that many of those caught up in this cult will be genuine believers in Christ. However, the reality of their faith will be weakened and their effectiveness for God could be destroyed by on-going contact with this cult.

## Our Response

1. We need to engage in serious and concerned prayer for people caught up in this cult.

2. We need to know what we believe and why. This means genuine and prolonged study of God's Word, the Bible.

3. We need to realize that severe psychological damage can be caused in those caught up in the movement for any length of time and so they desperately need to experience the compassion of Christ.

4. We need to be well-informed. If CLCOC can show that there is no truth in our allegations their cause is only helped. One former member said that the reason he had to listen to his family when they questioned him about his involvement with CLCOC was that they knew so much about it.

5. We need to be deeply sensitive and very patient with anyone we meet who has been involved with this cult and pray that we might lead them to the Saviour.

# Scientology

The leaders of the religious movement known as Scientology have made it a matter of policy to use the law to harass and sue people who criticize and expose them. Their founder stated: "The purpose of legal action is to harass, and discourage rather than to win. The law can be used very easily to harass." Scientologists are also assumed to have a sophisticated undercover operational arm, which steals documents and engages in spying, disinformation and dirty tricks. The American journalist, Paulette Cooper was 'persecuted' for writing critically about scientology. A smear campaign was organized against her. Private detectives followed her and anonymous letters were written to her neighbours accusing her of crimes against children. She was accused of making bomb threats against scientologists and of threatening the President and Secretary of State of the U.S.A. These threats were written on paper which contained her fingerprints as the paper had been stolen from her house. It took her 2 years and 24,000 dollars in costs to clear her name. Scientology seems to have a sinister and brutal aspect to its activities.

The British cult monitoring group "Family Action, Information and Rescue" (FAIR) recently analyzed the 2,911 calls for help that it had received during a period of twelve months. Of the 171 specific groups mentioned in that survey the number one trouble-making cult in Britain was Scientology.

It is enshrined in the UN charter articles 18 and 19 that we are free to believe whatever we wish in terms of philosophy and religion. This is a fundamental human right. However, we also have a right to examine and examine in depth what those beliefs and practices are, and to criticize, condemn and expose those doctrines which are untrue and/or dangerous.

## The Founder

The founder of Scientology was **Lafayette Ron Hubbard**, who was born in Tilden, Nebraska on 13th March 1911. He died of a stroke in 1986 and his remains were cremated. His grandfather was the town vet, while his father was in the navy and ended his career as Lieutenant commander. Hubbard travelled to Guam at the age of 16 and also lived in other places in the Far East when his father was stationed in the Pacific. Later he attended George Washington University but left after two years because of poor grades. Later he made a somewhat precarious living as a writer of science fiction, producing numerous items for science fiction magazines. During World War II he joined the navy, achieving the rank of first lieutenant. He was reprimanded for injudicious acts, but never took part in any action against the enemy. He left the navy suffering with an ulcer, conjunctivitis and arthritis, and received a small pension.

His first wife, Polly, with whom he had two children, Ron Junior and Katie, was abandoned for the girlfriend of his best friend Jack Parsons. She was called Sara Northrup and despite all that happened Hubbard and Parsons stayed friends. Parsons introduced Hubbard to the occult as he was a devotee of Aleister Crowley (The Beast). Hubbard went through a marriage ceremony with Sara, illegally as it turned out for he was not yet divorced from Polly. He continued his writing career but never earned enough money for the lifestyle he wanted. In 1950 he devised a new "science of the mind" and called it "Dianetics" or "science thought". His first book on Dianetics hit the bestseller lists and became the American craze of 1950. This book became the basis for the whole structure, which eventually Hubbard called "Scientology".

Hubbard separated from Sara who had a child by him called Alexis. It was a bitter split, with Sara accusing him of cruelty and torture. She later retracted those charges in order to obtain her child, whom Hubbard had kidnapped for four months.

His science was eventually "religionised" to help it gain charity status and tax avoidance. The money began accumulating and by the mid 1960s he was prospering financially. By then he was married to Mary Sue with whom he had four children.

In 1959 Hubbard moved to Saint Hill Manor, a large estate at East Grinstead in Sussex. This was the Headquarters for worldwide Scientology for the next eight years. He left in 1967 and for nearly ten years lived on a ship before going ashore permanently in the mid 1970s to live in Palm Springs. By now he was overweight, grey and had rotten teeth. Also he had been operated on to remove a large lump from his forehead, then he suffered heart attacks in 1975 and 1978.

In 1983 his wife served time in prison, this seems to have saved Hubbard from a similar fate, as the authorities investigated him for tax evasions and illegal activities. For the final years of his life he lived as a virtual recluse in hiding with an entourage of seven followers, and earning one million dollars a week.

Hubbard's relationship with some family members broke down: His son Ron Junior dropped out of scientology in 1959. He turned against his father, branding him insane as Hubbard had a furious temper, obsessions about dust and dirt and a cruel system of punishments for disobedient followers. Hubbard also refused to meet Alexis, claiming she was the daughter of Jack Parsons and his son Quentin killed himself in 1976. This seemed to have been more embarrassing than distressing to his father. Hubbard died in 1986, but the "Church of Scientology" far from ceasing, continues and flourishes better than ever before.

## The Church of Scientology

Scientology is defined in Collins Concise Dictionary as: "A cult founded in the early 1950s based upon the belief that self-awareness is paramount, that believes in reincarnation." The booklet, *Scientology: What is it?* published by the Church of Scientology International (1985) says: "Scientology is a study of...the very basic knowledge about man and about life that is vital for each person to have if he is to be happy and accomplish those things he sets out to do...The application of Scientology principles can improve a person's confidence, intelligence, abilities and skills... Scientology steers the individual out of the problems and seeming restrictions of everyday life, to a point where he can gain higher levels of spiritual freedom." Hubbard defined scientology as "The study of knowledge in its fullest sense."

Scientology has numerous organizations associated with it:

Author Service Incorporated

Advanced Organization Saint Hill

Bridge Publications (Los Angeles)

Concerned Businessmen's Association of the UK

Narconon

New Era Publications (Copenhagen)

Saint Hill Foundation

Sea Org

Way to Happiness Campaign

Its periodicals include: *Advance, Auditor, Crusader* and *Freedom.*

The cult essentially started in 1950 with the publication of the book: *Dianetics: the Modern Science of Mental Health* by L. Ron Hubbard. *Dianetics* promised help for people to overcome all irrational behaviour, compulsions, repressions and psychosomatic illnesses. The end result being not everlasting life, but an extended and happy life.

Initially scientology was not seen as a religion but as a science. Scientology does not involve worship to any deity, nor did it originally include any regular meetings for worship. The Church of Scientology of California was incorporated on 18th February 1954 and meetings for worship were added but few scientologists attend. Hubbard rejected Christianity completely. He denied the fact of heaven and initially denied that Jesus lived. However, in later life he admitted that Jesus had lived but claimed that he was gay! The roots of scientology lie in the fertile imagination of L. Ron Hubbard.

Those interested in scientology are encouraged to fill in a free personality analysis form containing 200 questions. The results of the analysis can only be obtained at a scientology centre on a pre-arranged appointment date. From this, courses in self-awareness and personal development are offered, but these have to be paid for.

The essence of scientology belief is as follows:

1. Each person is an immortal soul, known as a **"thetan"**. This makes repeated journeys to earth to adopt different bodies. Thetans are powerful beings having created everything, but their power is diminished by **"engrams"**.

2. **"Engrams"** are traumatic experiences, which cause physical, emotional and mental problems. Engrams may be accidental (e.g. resulting from inter-galactic wars) or **"implants"**.

3. **"Implants"** these are deliberately inflicted by other thetans who want power. The results may be illness, insanity and apathy. What is needed is **"auditing"**.

4. **"Auditing"** is aimed at getting rid of **"engrams"** and neutralizing "implants". To be rid of engrams makes a scientologist **"clear"**.

5. **"Clear"** means to be free from **"engrams"**. This apparently is measurable by an **"E-meter"**. Thus a **"clear"** is "the optimum individual, no longer possessed of any engrams" (Hubbard).

6. The **"E-meter"** (or electropsychometer) supposedly checks if any engrams are present. It works in a similar way to a simple lie detector.

Scientology now has two huge dictionaries with over 1,000 pages of words and phrases.

**"Auditing"** is an amalgam of psychotherapy and the Catholic confession. People explore past problems, which of itself may be therapeutic and makes them feel good. They attribute this to Scientology and are hooked. Hypnosis may also be used and a light trance euphoria is produced which feeds the desire for more experiences and so people become dependent upon scientology. Such relatively simple beginnings lead on to more bizarre fantasies reminiscent of the science fiction writer. Higher levels talk of landing stations on Venus, of Xenu who controlled 76 planets, 75 million years ago and implanted captured thetans with religion, sexual perversions and other ideas, which are found in people today. This apparently explains where these ideas originated and scientologists who reach 'Operating Theton 3' are taught to rid themselves of such ideas.

As a young man Hubbard was apparently fond of saying that the quickest way to make a million was to start a religion. He has proved this to be correct and scientology does not come cheaply. It costs £150,000 to undertake full scientology training and only a few hundred followers worldwide, have made it "up the bridge" as far as they can go. Someone has described Scientology as "Up the Neverending Bridge" because on completion of one course another awaits you. Hubbard claimed that he took only a modest salary and that he signed over royalties to Scientology. This is contradicted by the fact that he left over 500 million dollars at his death. Those taking courses are told to keep it secret and never to discuss it with outsiders. This enhances the mystique and sense of exclusiveness, which Scientology engenders. There may be up to one million Scientologists world wide, though the church has claimed several million adherents. It is still a large cult for one founded in the twentieth century.

In the mid 1960s Scientology introduced an "ethics" code on followers and an "ethics" officer to police it. This system imposed punishments known as '**conditions**' upon students or workers in the organization who were either: suspected of being lazy, disloyal and breaking rules or failing to increase productivity which was measured in points.

The '**conditions**' imposed were:

1. A grey rag tied around the arm, so that all knew who was in disgrace.

2. Depriving the individual of sleep for up to 84 hours.

3. Declaring someone a suppressive person (SP). This was the ultimate sanction.

When someone was declared an "SP" the "Fair Game Law" came into operation. Suppressive persons were not only excommunicated but became fair game for every kind of harassment at each opportunity. Thus they can be "tricked, sued, lied to and destroyed".

In 1967 Hubbard left Britain and established "Sea Org", the floating branch of scientology. He crossed the Mediterranean and Caribbean seas in three ships, with his wife rarely with him on the same ship. He was known as "commodore" and was surrounded by "commodore messengers" who were mainly female teenagers. Scientology parents felt honoured to have their children serve Hubbard in this way. These messengers laid out his clothes, lit his cigarettes (he smoked 80 a day), followed him with ashtrays, ran his shower and cleaned his room. In return they received a pittance and were screamed at if work was not up to standard. "Conditions" were imposed upon any who failed on board ship. Thus work was hard, hours long and the food poor. Yet money was pouring into the organization as it advertised, pressured for donations and continued the flow of books and literature.

As a result of the activities of this cult considerable opposition has built up against it. One survey conducted in 1981 showed that:

1. A higher percentage (35%) of scientologists had received physical punishment than any other cult members.

2. It took ex-members longer to recover from this cult's mind control than those of other cults.

3. Ex-members have the highest rates of sexual dysfunctions, violent outbursts, hallucinations, delusions and suicidal tendencies than those of other cults.

An Australian Government Inquiry in 1965 concluded: "Scientology is evil, its techniques are evil, its practice is a serious threat to the community, medically, morally, and socially; and its adherents are sadly deluded and often medically ill."

In 1984 David Alton, a former Liberal M.P. for Liverpool Mossley Hill, and a Roman Catholic, introduced a 10-minute rule bill to give the Home Secretary powers to ban organizations which were found to be using underhand methods such as brainwashing, corrupting and dubious methods to obtain money. He said: "These cults are spreading their evil influence all over Britain. I want legislation to control the activities of these pseudo-religious gangsters."

A high court judge, Mr. Justice Latey wrote that in his judgment: "auditing is a process of conditioning, brainwashing and indoctrination." He went on to say: "Discipline is ruthless and obedience has to be unquestioning...Scientology must come before family and friends...it is corrupt, sinister and dangerous. It is corrupt because it is based on lies and deceit and has as its real objective money and power...It is sinister because it indulges in infamous practices both to its adherents who do not toe the line unquestioningly, and to those who criticize or oppose it. It is dangerous because it is out to capture people, especially children and impressionable young people and indoctrinate and brainwash them so that they become the unquestioning captives and tools of the cult, withdrawn from ordinary thought, living and relating with others."

## Present Situation

On Hubbard's death in 1986, David Miscavige took control at the age of 25. He had been a messenger since the age of 17 and had been seen as Ron Hubbard's mouthpiece. He engineered a clearing out of senior officials, many of long-standing and there was a general reorganization. This was more complicated by the fact that the sole executor of Hubbard's estate and trust was Norman Starkey. To hang on to the 500 million dollar estate he has founded the Church of Spiritual Technology.

Money continues to pour in and each organization is worth over 500 million dollars. The Church of Scientology continues to avoid the US tax authorities by making its headquarters a ship called *Freewinds* which sails the Caribbean, outside territorial waters. It carries the scientology elite who come to take the most advanced courses, paying 15,000 dollars a week for the privilege. All is protected by guards and cameras. There are 280 crew members, all scientologists, who work hard, earn less tham 50 dollars a week and have signed a contract for a million years. This commitment is to be honoured on pain of total banishment from the church forever – so they remain loyal.

The US Judge Brechenbridge when he dismissed a case that the scientologists had brought against an ex-member said: "In addition to violating and abusing its own members' civil rights, the organization has over the years...harassed and abused those persons not in the church whom it perceives as enemies. The organization clearly is schizophrenic and paranoid and this bizarre combination seems to be a reflection of its founder LRH. The evidence (in this case) portrays a man who has been virtually a pathological liar when it comes to his history, background and achievements. The writings and documents in evidence additionally reflect his egoism, greed, avarice, lust for power and vindictiveness and aggressiveness against persons perceived by him to be disloyal and hostile."

# Therapy EST

EST has been advertised as "A powerful and practical inquiry into the issues that determine our personal effectiveness." The late singer John Denver was reputed to have said of his EST encounters, "It is the single most important experience of my life."

EST is a "therapy cult" and these are more difficult to identify than religious cults as they tend to be aimed at personal self-improvement and potential realization. They do not gather for worship, do not have a 'theology' and do not own local buildings for services. They often claim not to have members. This may be true in a formal sense but they do acquire a following and often radical personal and emotional changes take place in those who become involved with them.

Other therapy cults include: PSI Mind Development Institute; Scientology; School of Economic Science; Mind Awareness; Lifespring; Lifestream and Exegesis.

The letters EST stand for Erhard Seminar Training, though it has also been pointed out that the letters spell the Latin word for "it is". Today the name has been changed to "The Centres Network" which organize "The Forum", essentially a series of courses and seminars. These are advertised as non-religious, self-help training sessions that are designed to bring participants to fulfillment. EST teach that you are your own god and that everything you experience is a product of your own divine creative will. It claims that the only reality exists in the individual's mind.

## The Founder

The founder **Werner Erhard** born in 1935, started life with the name **John Paul Rosenberg**. He came from Philadelphia and was apparently preoccupied with concerns about guilt, predestination and God as the result of a near-drowning and fractured skull suffered in childhood. He married at the age of 18, but finally abandoned his wife and four children in the early 1960's. He eloped to California with another woman, and in an attempt to hide his identity he changed his name to Erhard. For 13 years he worked as a car salesman, seller of correspondence courses and trainer of encyclopaedia sellers. He also explored Zen Buddhism, Scientology, Silva Mind Control and hypnosis which all became the basis for his teaching in EST.

In March 1971 he claimed that he had "got it" while driving down a California highway. "I became Self", he said. In Autumn 1971 he held his first Erhard Seminar Training Course at a San Francisco hotel with 1,000 participants. Since then over half a million 'graduates' have gone through the training.

His second wife Ellen Erhard divorced him after 22 years of marriage. She apparently said that "Werner's ego and public image are the most important things in the world to him." Ellen Erhard's claim to half the property of EST may have been a significant factor in bringing about the major shake up in the organization that included its new name. There was also a need to revamp and significantly alter the image for a new generation, as there had been a decline in enrolment.

## The Extent of EST

Courses are expensive and usually take place over two consecutive weekends. Thus four days are involved (2 Saturdays and 2 Sundays). Each lasts from 9.00 a.m. to 11.30 p.m., as well as one 3-hour evening session. The goal of EST is 'getting it'. Erhard says: "We want nothing short of a total transformation - an alteration of substance, not a change of form". Across the world, an estimated 6,000 people per month do the training and many go back for refresher courses. The course is run three or four times a year in Britain with as many as 200 attending each one. Most complete the full course, especially as they have made an enormous commitment of time and money and are not prepared to admit, even to themselves, that the whole thing was a waste of time.

Research in America has suggested that candidates who attend EST courses are over-whelmingly white, middle class and well educated. However, they tend to have a lower than average income, with two thirds being unmarried, divorced or separated. It may be that these recruits tend to be sixties dropouts who are trying to reconcile the idealism of youth with the changed circumstances of middle age when they have had to drop back into society. It may also reflect deep dissatisfaction by people who have failed to become high achievers and failed to have long-standing relationships.

## The Philosophy of EST

The method of approach is disorientation technique. Sessions take place in rooms with no natural light, no clocks and with few breaks for toilet or food and the trainees are broken down with verbal brutality. It is an authoritarian, confrontational style of approach that can produce psychological damage to a group of people who may already be stressed. However as a result of adverse publicity Centres Network has now suggested that those who want to under-go therapy should get their own therapist's permission before going on a course.

The techniques have been refined over the years and are now less aggressive, but still the aim is to make the trainee dependent upon the trainer. After these courses most participants are emotionally, physically and mentally exhausted, while some are permanently traumatized. The *American Journal of Psychiatry* (1977) presented seven cases of psychiatric disturbance as the result of EST, only one of which had a previous history of psychiatric trouble.

The aim seems to be to shred and destroy a person's belief system and replace it with the teaching of EST. Trainees are taught that they are three persons:

The person they pretend to be.

The person they fear they really are.

The real self.

The aim is to reach the real self (i.e. "getting it").

Erhard's worldview of life is a sort of perfection with no difference between right and wrong, as he indicated when he wrote, "Wrong is actually a version of right. If you are always wrong you are right." So he admits to no absolutes, no objective truth, except the absolute that: "Whatever is, is right". Thus it could be argued that anyone has the right to do whatever he wishes, including indiscriminate killing.

Erhard's view is that God is man and man is God, and that each individual must come to understand he is his own God. "I can do anything. One of these days, I'll be so complete I won't be human, I'll be

God." (John Denver) This, of course, means that we can do as we please, since as God we are answerable to no one. Also the need to look to a Supreme Being for salvation is gone and the God of the Bible is unnecessary. Indeed Erhard sees belief in God as the greatest barrier to the experience of God! EST denies the basic beliefs of the historic Christian faith, yet claims compatibility with Jesus Christ and Christianity! They say that Christ said the same sort of things as Erhard, so there is no need to give Jesus any special adoration.

"...The church totally misinterpreted what Jesus said. He kept telling over and over that everybody was like He was, perfect. He was experiencing life, like Werner. He knew He was the total source, living moment by moment, and was spontaneous. Jesus is just another guru who happens to be popular here in Western Civilization. I can't go into a church and praise Jesus. But I really got where he is coming from. He wants to let everybody know "I'm you". So my whole point of view about religion has totally altered." (EST publication quoted in *Understanding the Cults.*)

"The entire EST system centres around the self-centred individual rather than the Biblical God. In EST, God is non-existent...The experience EST offers is a pseudo-answer to man's deepest need." (McDowell & Stewart)

**Other Aspects**

There have been court cases against EST by those who claim that EST caused them emotional distress and mental breakdown. The Inland Revenue has also investigated their tax situation.

Erhard claimed that his work has been woven into

the fabric of American culture. "You see the language from our work in business and advertising." (Erhard) Indeed many business organizations have sent their people to the seminar programmes to improve on their communication, relationship and productivity skills. Many graduates claim to have experienced a revolution in their lives by attending EST seminars. However, concern has been expressed over the pressure and intensity of the programmes.

Erhard, together with John Denver set up in 1977 an organization called "The Hunger Project"! This is a charity that aims to eliminate world hunger. Though supposedly not connected with EST, a large proportion of the staff is EST trained and those on EST training weekends are encouraged to support the project. It also has a young people's wing known as "Youth Ending Hunger". This project has had a large profile. It attracted for a while the backing of ex-prime minister Edward Heath. It was nearly accepted on an official basis by Birmingham Local Education Authority as part of its education to schools programme. Had it been accepted and promoted in the 500 schools of Birmingham it would have received great credibility and other education authorities would have been under pressure to accept it.

The problem with the "Hunger Project" is that it does not actually feed the hungry. Nor does it claim to. Only one half of one per cent of its British income and just over 2 percent of its international income is spent on food for the hungry. The project is founded on the EST belief that what the world needs to do to eliminate hunger is to wake up to the fact that there is a hunger problem, and that if we all talk about it enough, we will create a climate in which hunger can no longer exist!

## Final Observations

– No one is forced to go on EST courses and many leave before they complete the courses.

– Many are grateful for what they have experienced on EST courses.

–EST tends to encourage focus on "self". It is inward looking with more concern for "me" than for others.

–The courses can lead to dependency upon EST as the need for refresher courses indicate.

–The experience of "getting it" is a pseudo experience and not a lasting, eternal transformation.

–The teaching of EST is non-Christian, even anti-Christian.

–EST is incompatible with genuine Christianity.

–EST now forms part of the new age network.

–EST has produced profound emotional, physical, psychological and certainly spiritual problems in many who attend the courses.

Believing Christians need to pray that by the grace of God others will be reached before therapy cults influence them and the barrier towards the Gospel of Jesus Christ then becomes greater.

# Islam

Today the followers of Islam number about one billion and are the majority religion in over fifty countries. These include the North African nations, the Middle Eastern nations and nations in South Asia, including some of the states of Central Asia which were part of the former Soviet bloc. The most populous Islamic country is Indonesia. Islam is an expansionist religion and spends considerable sums of money on mission activities. It has made considerable inroads into Africa, south of the Sahara, and into the West. Over 10 million Muslims live in the West, roughly evenly divided between those who live in the USA and those who live in Europe. Islam is spreading rapidly amongst black Americans and amongst West Indians and Africans in Britain. It is estimated that 70,000 Caucasians turned to Islam in the USA in the decade 1973 –1983.

In many ways Islam is a very aggressive religion and actively discriminates against Christians and even legally endorses their persecution. In Saudi Arabia any citizen who becomes a Christian faces the death penalty. Accusations of blasphemy against the prophet Muhammad are capital offences in Pakistan. Communal violence has martyred thousands of Christian believers in Nigeria and Indonesia. Also Muslim fundamentalist groups try to subvert the political processes in many countries and attempt to gain control, so that they can impose the strict Islamic (*Shari'ah*) law code, which discriminates against non-Muslims and even denies them basic civil rights. Education and the media are also widely used to deride Christianity and undermine its truth.

## History

The religion was founded by the prophet **Muhammad** who was born in Mecca in AD 570. As a youth he made contact with Jews and Christians and discussed religious matters with them, especially in terms of the Old and New Testament. This seems to have produced the basis for his passionate conviction that there is only one true God and made him react against the polytheism and idol worship he found in Mecca. In AD 595 he married a wealthy widow named Khadijah and her wealth enabled him to spend the next 15 years in seclusion and meditation. During this time he claimed to receive visions from the angel Gabriel and became convinced that he was a prophet of God. His family and a few sympathisers became his early followers, but the authorities in Mecca persecuted him and an attempt was made on his life.

He fled to Medina in AD 622 and this flight (*the Hijira*) marks the turning point in Islam's history and all Islamic calendars mark this date as their beginning. Accepted in Medina, Muhammad became an able administrator and also learnt that the sword was a more powerful weapon than the word. He eventually attacked and took control of Mecca, destroyed its idols and consecrated the famous black stone of Mecca (*the Ka'abah*) as the centre of Islamic worship. Since then Islam has expanded and Muslims have not been afraid to use force to compel conversions.

The official Islamic book is *the Qur'an*, a word that

means "recitation" or "reading". It is divided into 114 chapters *(suras)* and was written by the followers of the prophet as they remembered his utterances. It was written in Arabic and was revised and standardised in the 7th century and translations are actively discouraged. The *Qur'an* is supplemented to a very great extent by traditions (*Hadith*) which are the words and actions of Muhammad and his followers that have been handed down through the generations.

## Beliefs

Islam teaches that there is one God and his name is Allah. This is clearly not the God of the Bible, as it is not possible to know this God personally. He is characterised by judgement and power, but not by mercy and grace. Angels are important in Islam, firstly because they reputedly brought the revelation to Muhammad, and secondly each person is believed to have two angels, one recording the good deeds and the other the bad. Followers of Islam believe that God has spoken through many prophets, the greatest of whom were Adam, Noah, Abraham, Moses, Jesus and Muhammad, with the latter being the last and greatest. Islamic followers look forward to a time of resurrection and judgement when all those that follow and obey Allah and Muhammad will go to a place of pleasure called Paradise, while all others will be tormented in hell. Islam also has a rigid view of predestination that states that all good and evil come from the divine will. This has produced the common Islamic phrase, "It is Allah's will".

As far as family life is concerned, there is an expectation that everyone will marry and a man may have up to four wives and as many concubines as he can maintain. He may divorce his wife at any time and for any reason, though women have no right of divorce.

They consider Jesus to be both a prophet and a messenger of Allah and believe in his virgin birth and ability to perform miracles. They deny His deity and His crucifixion, for they do not believe that Allah would allow an innocent man to suffer for the sins of others. They believe that Jesus was translated into heaven before dying and someone else was substituted on the cross. Also the promise that Jesus gave to His followers, of a Comforter to come, is interpreted in Islam as a prediction of the coming of Muhammad.

### The Five Pillars of Islam

Islam teaches that works as well as faith are necessary for salvation. So "Islam" which means "submission to God" is practised in terms of fulfilling "the five principles" or "five pillars of faith".

**1. The Confession of Faith** (*the Kalima*). This consists of a creed spoken in Arabic, which means: "There is no god but Allah" and is usually followed by, "and Muhammad is the prophet of Allah". This is the bedrock of Islamic belief and one must state this aloud publicly in order to become a Muslim. It is repeated regularly by the faithful.

**2. The Ritual of Daily Prayer** (*the Salat*). Muslim prayers consist of reciting in Arabic prescribed words, while performing certain gestures and prostrations. There are five obligatory times for prayer and the faithful would never miss them. These take place at dawn, noon, late afternoon, sunset and at the end of twilight. There is ceremonial cleansing before prayers and the prayers are recited while facing Mecca.

**3. The Ramadan Fast** (*the Sawn*). This fast lasts from sunrise to sunset each day during the holy ninth month of Ramadan. Muhammad declared that it was during this month that the *Qur'an* began to be revealed from heaven. To keep the fast is to help in the process of forgiveness and to show in a public way the attachment of people to their religious community.

**4. The Giving of Alms** (*the Zakat*). Having experienced life as an orphan the prophet had a strong desire to help the needy. Today a religious tax is imposed and is said to help purify both the giver and his property from evil. It is also widely viewed as increasing spiritual merit and earning the forgiveness of sins.

**5. The Pilgrimage to Mecca** (*the Hajj*). Every Muslim is required to go to Mecca at least once in their lifetime. Over a million assemble in the city every year and this heightens their sense of Islamic solidarity.

There is also a sixth religious duty known as *the Jihad* or Holy War. When situations warrant it men are required to go to war to spread Islam or defend it against unbelievers. If one dies in a *Jihad* there is promise of eternal life in paradise.

## Gospel Outreach

Today Christian churches are found in nearly every country of the world, including the Muslim countries and there has been an increase in the number of Muslims turning to Christ. We need to pray that this process will accelerate and also be prepared to encourage every means for spreading the Gospel. Today this is done through Gospel radio broadcasts, Bible correspondence courses, evangelisation of ethnic communities in the West and Christians who take up secular jobs enabling them to enter the Muslim world and utilise informal opportunities of presenting the message of salvation through faith in Christ. In view of Islam's fierce opposition to the truth of the Gospel, Muslims will only be reached effectively when the work is done under God's leading, in accordance with His word and in dependence upon the power of His Holy Spirit.

# The Occult

The word "occult" derives from the Latin word for "hidden", "secret" or "mysterious" and concerns the unseen powers and activities of demons who are controlled by their master the Devil. In the New Testament there are over eighty references to demons and the Lord Jesus taught very clearly that demons are real and have extensive power. Thus Scripture bears witness to the reality of occult activity and many missionaries have affirmed this truth from their own experience. Raymond Buker who served the Lord for sixteen years in Burma, wrote, "Those of us who have served on mission fields are aware of the reality of demonic activities. Many of us have seen demon-possessed people in action."

## Occult Activity

In contemporary Western society there has been a phenomenal increase in occultic activity. There are estimated to be over 2,000 occult sects in France, with over 70,000 fortune-tellers, clairvoyants and astrologers. Britain has not been immune and media reports, together with personal experiences strongly indicate that occult practices are on the increase. The following are reasons for this increasing interest:

1. The meaningless dissatisfaction with life in a materialistic, hedonistic society. When every material and physical need is met and people are satiated with

entertainment, then man confronts the empty void of his own existence and seeks answers in a variety of places including the occult.

2.  Eastern religious practices have heavily infiltrated the West and these are anchored directly in the occult and spirit world.

3.  The weakness of evangelical Christianity in presenting the Gospel in a relevant and effective way. The result is that society sees no answer or power in the message of the Bible and has largely ignored it, often turning to the occult for its answers.

4.  Much occult activity is commercially driven. The ready availability of do-it-yourself séance kits, ouija board games, occult games such as "Dungeon and Dragons", together with the many books, films and videos devoted to the occult give many people the opportunity to enter the doorway into the demonic world.

5.  Fascination with the mysterious, with television programmes such as the "X files", studies of UFOs and the strange powers of pyramids have developed deep interest in the occult for many people.

6.  The need to gain insights and knowledge about the future has encouraged people to dabble into the occult by consulting mediums and astrologers.

7.  The need for comfort at a time of bereavement has led some to consult occultic practitioners in the vain hope of making contact with the dead or affirming that their loved one is happily settled in a better place.

8.  The desire for power and knowledge has made some people seek it in the occult realm.

Demons appear to be fallen angels who serve Satan in his rebellion against God (Matt.12.24; 25.41). They do their utmost to disrupt, control, manipulate, oppress, depress and possess people. Thus it is a highly dangerous practice to get involved in any occult practice as the example of Legion makes clear in Mark 5. Legion was so controlled by demons that it had a horrendously oppressive effect upon his life, with the narrative indicating the following:

1. He was fascinated by death and lived in a graveyard. Today many occult practices take place in cemeteries.

2. He was physically affected and had an unnatural or supernatural strength. Men were powerless to control him, as he was able to break out of anything they used to bind him. Walter Martin gives the following example: "The girl who was about 5 feet 4 inches tall and weighed 120 pounds, attacked a 180 pound man and with one arm flipped him 5 or 6 feet away. It took four of us including her husband to hold her body to a bed while we prayed in the name of Jesus Christ."

3. He was emotionally affected and was seized with surges of great anger and violent rage.

4. He was mentally affected and he shouted and cut himself with stones. Legion experienced terrible inner pressures that produced self-destructive, even suicidal tendencies.

5. He had strange powers of understanding and clearly had a very profound knowledge of the person of Jesus Christ.

## Manifestations of the Occult

Today there are many manifestations of the occult of which the following are some of the most prominent:

**Witchcraft**: Since the "Repeal of Witchcraft Act" in 1959 witchcraft is not illegal in Britain, though that is not true of some of its practices. Witches (men and women) meet in groups called covens. They perform rites and ceremonies devoted to Satan, including chanting, dancing, animal sacrifices, possibly involving sexual activities and it has been suggested there may even be human sacrifices in some instances. These are done in secret places and may involve stone circles and fires and take place at special times of the year. Halloween is an important date in the occult calendar as it was the ancient Celtic "day of death" and marks the end of Autumn and the beginning of Winter. Satanic power is said to be at its greatest on October 31st.

**2. Astrology:** This is the attempt to explain how the lives of people and events on earth are controlled by the position of celestial bodies. The claim is made that one's life pattern is determined by the position of stars and planets at one's birth. No one explains why birth and not conception is so vital. Also the differing life experiences of twins is unexplained by astrology. There are also contradictory astrological systems and many are based on mediaeval systems that were formulated before the discovery of the planets Uranus, Neptune and Pluto. It is also noteworthy that the constellations change through time and are not static as astrology claims. Astrology encourages superstition and fatalism, leaving people open to more serious occult influences.

**3. Fortune telling:** This is the attempt to predict the future by divination. Such methods include palmistry or hand-reading, phrenology or interpretation of cranial bumps, iridology or eye-diagnosis, cartomancy or card cutting, pendulum swinging and teacup reading.

**4. Ouija boards:** "Ouija" means "Yes, Yes" in French and German. It is widely marketed as a game and is commonly known as "spirit in the glass". Forms of it were used as long ago as six centuries before Christ. Fingers are placed on the glass and the spirit is asked a question and moves to "Yes" or "No". Words are spelt and messages given. This 'harmless' fun game has caused many to have direct contact with the world of Satan.

**5. Satanism:** This is direct worship of Satan. Anton LeVey in San Francisco founded the first Satanic church. He wrote his own Satanic Bible, altered the Ten Commandments to say the opposite, practised all sorts of perversions, placed a cross upside down and draped an undressed young woman over an altar. He openly mocks God, the Lord Jesus and Christian truth.

## The Christian Position

God condemns all occult practice (Ex.22.18; Deut.18.9-14) His anger is directed against those who practice it (2 Chron. 33.6) and He wants everyone to leave it, avoid it and burn any occult effects we may possess (Isa. 47.9-15; Jer. 27.9-10; Acts 19.19). He wants us to trust Him and His Son, Jesus Christ. He knows the danger people place themselves in when they open up their lives to the occult. They allow Satan a foothold in their lives that may be exploited; it leaves people fearful and often with altered personalities. Such people have a much deeper resistance to the Gospel and find it hard to understand the Christian message. Ultimately those people can be led into destruction and the horror of the torment of hell.

It is interesting that Jesus never touched those who were demon-possessed. He commanded the demons to depart and in the missionary enterprise in the book of Acts demons were ejected at "the name of Jesus" (Acts 16.18; 19.13-18). Today it is never wise to seek a ministry in this area, unless the Lord clearly brings someone across your path. It is important to keep close to the Lord through prayer and maintenance of a clean life. The only authority we have is the name of the Lord Jesus and His Word.

Satan is a real enemy who is both strong and subtle. He can even attack and discourage Christian people. Yet we must remember, that "Greater is He that is in you (that's the Lord), than he that is in the world (that is Satan)" (1 John 4.4). Also if we submit ourselves to God we will be able to resist the Devil and he will flee from us (James 4.7). We are in an intensive and serious spiritual battle but ultimately Christ is victorious and through his death on the cross Satan is already defeated and his destiny and doom are assured (Rev. 20.10). We praise God that through the shed blood of Christ many are being delivered from Satan's bondage today.

# Astrology

Astrology has been called "The foolish daughter of a wise mother - astronomy". Astronomy is the scientific study of the stars, planets and galaxies. Astrology is a superstition with occult connections that can lead to fatalism.

Today those who write and publish astrology earn a great deal of money. Horoscopes are seen in newspapers and magazines, they are part of media presentations on radio and television and there are whole shelves full of astrological books in most bookshops. It has been said that "Astrology enjoys a popularity today unmatched since the decline of Rome." Researcher, Bernard Gittelson has calculated that the circulation of newspapers and magazines carrying astrological columns in the U.S.A., Europe, Japan and South America is over 700 million.

A 1975 poll in the U.S.A. indicated that 32 million Americans believed "that the stars influence people's lives". In 1984 a poll among 13-18 year olds revealed that 55% of U.S. teenagers believed in astrology. A more disturbing poll in 1988 indicated that 10% of evangelicals in the U.S. believe in astrology.

It is estimated that there are over 10,000 full-time astrologers and 175,000 part-timers in the U.S.A. Today there are over 100 magazines devoted to astrology in the West, millions of books are in print, and since 1960 the annual production of new titles has doubled every ten years. Apparently every area of human experience can have astrology applied to it: there are horoscopes for dogs, cats, fish, babies, teenagers, cooking, diet and health, finance, sex, medicine, earthquake prediction, politics and so on. Over 80% of U.S. newspapers carry horoscope columns and the names of those who consult the stars include members of the Royal Family, actors like Robert Wagner, Roger Moore and previously Steve McQueen, actresses like Joan Collins, Liza Minnelli, Jane Fonda, Olivia Newton-John, Goldie Hawn, Lauren Bacall, Jill St. John and many more. Former White House Chief of Staff, Donald T. Regan in his book *For the Record,* wrote that the influence of astrology during the Reagen administration extended to "every major move and decision".

Astrology is offered as courses in some schools and colleges and is possibly as much as a one billion dollar a year industry. CNN reported that at least 300 of the Fortune 500 companies use astrologers in one way or another.

## What is Astrology?

Astrology is the belief that the stars and planets in some mysterious way influence our own planet and the lives of people. Astrology teaches that this influence begins at birth and continues through a person's life. Thus it is believed that the macro (universe) affects the micro (human beings).

Astrology has its roots in the ancient times when men worshipped the heavenly bodies as gods, but it reached its modern form around 140 A.D. under the guidance of Ptolemy. He assumed that the earth was the centre of the universe and concocted a complex system based upon the sky as it was visible in his day.

Though extremely involved astrology is made up of three main factors: the signs, the houses and the planets.

The **signs** are called the Zodiac signs or sun-signs. These are the divisions of a belt of sky into which the ancients built imaginary human and animal figures. There are twelve signs such as Libra, Gemini, Pisces, and each one corresponds to one twelfth of a year.

The **houses** are twelve sections of the Zodiac which symbolize aspects of life. For example the first house may represent personality, the second money, and so on.

The **planets** move through these houses and are significant for their position at the time of birth.

To picture this we need to imagine a clear glass globe, with a small marble in the middle which represents the earth. Around the globe is a thin white belt representing the Zodiac and divided into the 12 signs. From the marble come 12 sections or houses and it is through the sections that the planets are supposed to move.

In addition, the "**aspect**" is important and this is determined by the angles between planets. All this is plotted on a chart or map, which is called a horoscope, and from this your life and future can be plotted when such a chart is given at birth. Birth is the significant time and so astrology's vital need for information is the horoscope at birth.

The Greeks and Romans adopted this system and it developed in popularity during the Middle Ages. The rationalism of the 18th century and the scientific and industrial development of the 19th and early 20th century reduced interest in astrology to a very low ebb. However, it has not only survived but become an integral part of life in the last part of the 20th century and into the 21st century.

**Reasons for the Popularity of Astrology**

"History has shown that astrology thrives best in times of religious decline and of social unrest" *(Seattle Daily Times,* Sept. 1975). This seems to be true for when Rome was in decline citizens turned to astrology, while the turbulence and darkness of the Middle Ages led people to seek for answers and hope in astrology. The fear and uncertainty of our own days encourage many to seek meaning in the stars.

Other reasons are as follows:

1. The publicity given by horoscope columns in newspapers. This constant forecasting has persuaded many that the stars influence human destinies.

2. People have a basic need to believe in something. In our generation the certainties of spiritual and moral truth are being questioned, so people use astrology as a substitute for true faith.

3. Astrology is firmly rooted in eastern, mystical religions and these have infiltrated very deeply into Western society, leading to increased interest in astrology.

4. Astrology appears to offer a unity of meaning, an explanation in a world which seems to be falling apart and increasingly confused.

5. Astrology relieves people of accountability. It teaches that a person is what he or she is because of the influences of the planets and stars. This is set at birth and his subsequent life is on a preordained course. Such a belief is called fate.

6. A growing fear that science, politics, education, religion and government do not have the answers.

7. A horoscope seems easy to grasp in comparison with science or even some religious concepts.

8. Astrology is usually vague and general in its predictions and can be open to a number of

interpretations, any one of which may satisfy an individual.

9. An astrological chart seems very impressively worked out and even appear scientific and this may encourage many to believe that it is true.

## Inconsistencies with Astrology

Inherent in astrology are a number of inconsistencies:

1. **Conflicting Systems:** There are many systems of astrology that are often diametrically opposed to each other. There is a great difference between the interpretation of horoscopes in the West and those of Chinese astrologers. Even in the West there is no agreement as some astrologers see 8, or 14, or even 24 zodiac signs as opposed to 12.

2. **Geocentric Theory:** This was the original idea that the earth was the centre of the universe. However, in 1543 Copernicus discovered that the earth and planets revolve around the sun. This means that the reliability of astrology is destroyed, as the basic assumption is false and all conclusions are likewise false.

3. **Missing Planets:** In ancient times the astrologers had to view the sky with the naked eye and based their systems upon seven planets (the sun and moon were included). Since then three other planets have been discovered: Uranus in 1781, Neptune in 1839 and Pluto in 1932. Since all the planets are supposed to influence human life the system breaks down as these three are not usually considered.

4. **Twins**: A constant problem to an astrologer is that people born in the same place and at the same time can develop widely varying lifestyles.

5. **Birth only:** There is no logical reason why birth should be the significant moment for astrology to

influence a human life. Why not conception? No doubt the reason is that conception is extremely difficult to particularize.

6. **Opposition of Science:** In 1975, 186 leading scientists including 18 Nobel prize winners publicly disavowed astrology. Scientific opinion seems to be unanimous: "There is no evidence that astrology has any value...and there is not the slightest reason for believing that...events can be predicted by astrology." (*American Society for Psychological Research*)

7. **Shifting Constellations:** This is a process called precession. The signs which correspond to constellations 2,000 years ago cannot be the same as they are today, because constellations have shifted 30 degrees. Thus the constellation of Virgo is in the sign of Libra and so on.

8. **Prediction Failure:** Many times astrological predictions have been proved wrong.

**Dangers of Astrology**

1. It can be very expensive to buy all the paraphernalia and to pay for consultancy when astrology is taken seriously.

2 Astrological advice on investments, spending and purchasing is often wrong and can be costly.

3. Astrology is deterministic and can lead to a fatalistic view of life, which can induce real depression.

4. It can be life or health threatening as when women refuse medical advice to induce a baby because they want the child to be born under a later sign.

5. Most seriously of all astrology is strongly linked with the occult. Sybil Leek in her book: *My Life in Astrology* states: "Astrology is my science, witchcraft is my religion". Most occultists use astrology and many astrologers practice other occult arts. "Astrology is

essentially a magical art" (Richard Cavendish). Astrology is "found virtually everywhere occultism is to be found". (Dr John Warwick Montgomery).

6. Astrology is sometimes seen as 'soft' occult, relatively harmless in itself but providing a gateway for people to enter into 'hard' occult. It encourages superstition, creates receptiveness in the mind to other occult influences and generally weakens people's desire for God and appreciation of God.

## The Bible and Astrology

Nowhere in the Bible is there support for or encouragement given to the practice of astrology. In fact the opposite is the case. In Deuteronomy 17 v.2-5 the seriousness of worshipping the heavenly beings or of being involved with astrology called forth the death penalty. Isaiah 47 v.8-15 reveals that for all the predictions the astrologers and all their advice the judgment of God will surely, come and they will be quite helpless to prevent it. God is not subject to the movements of planets or the laws of nature. God is free to act as He wants. Thus astrology is an inadequate substitute for true revelation from God. Other warnings against astrology are given in Jeremiah 10 v.2 and Deuteronomy 4 v.19, while Daniel ch. 2 exposes the astrologers as ridiculous, futile, false and evil.

The early church opposed astrology, encouraging converts to burn their astrological equipment as in Acts 19 v.18-20. The church council in 345 A.D. held at Laodicia declared astrology forbidden. St. Augustine who had believed in astrology before he was converted, on becoming a Christian disavowed and opposed astrology. Protestant reformers followed this position and in Protestant countries astrology was forbidden by law and condemned by the church.

Today Christians need to be very wary. Astrology must have no influence over us, but in opposing the practice of astrology we must be very careful to demonstrate the compassion of Christ. It is not a crusade against astrology that we need today, but a Spirit-anointed proclamation of the Gospel of Jesus Christ. This alone will show the empty and valueless nature of astrology and reveal the deep fulfillment that Christ can give.

## One Final Point

Some astrologers have argued that the wisemen mentioned in Matthew ch.2 were astrologers and found their way to the child Jesus by means of a horoscope.

In response we can point out five factors. Firstly, it has to be said that, "there are no astrological allusions in this passage". (Boa)  Secondly, the star was not a conjunction of planets as it moved, appeared, disappeared, reappeared and remained stationary. This is hardly the behaviour of a planet or star and was most likely a phenomenon put there supernaturally by God. Thirdly, it is highly possible that these men were Gentile converts to Judaism and were familiar with Numbers 24 v.17: "A star will come out of Jacob...". This prophecy was always seen as referring to Messiah. Fourthly, King Herod did not view the wisemen as astrologers for he called, not his own astrologers, but scholars in the Old Testament to determine where Christ should be born. Finally, the wisemen did not use astrology to determine Herod's evil intentions. They were warned by an angel of God (Matthew 2 v.12). There is no mention of horoscopes in the passage.

# The New Age Movement –
# A Leaderless but Powerful Network

It was incredible to read that in the early 1990s a lady gave up her £150.00 per day job in the City of London, to take up work at the Findhorn Foundation in Scotland for £75.00 per month! Findhorn was the first New Age community in the world, being founded in 1962 and has achieved legendary status in New Age circles. There are now many more such communities of environmentally friendly housing, which offer ongoing programmes on the principles of New Age spirituality.

The New Age Movement (NAM) is said to be the fastest growing belief system in America and possibly in the Western world. It has infiltrated society so deeply that it is virtually impossible to escape its all-pervasive nature. Many people accept its thinking without realising it and NAM teaching has been popularised by well-known stars of film and stage such as John Denver and Shirley Maclaine. The latter's autobiographical book, *Out on a Limb* detailed her New Age philosophy.

## Background

In 1875 the Theosophical Society was founded and this has given a philosophical framework for NAM thinking. It linked Eastern religious thought to Western occultism and was violently opposed to monotheism.

Also in the turbulent 1960s many disaffected young people were introduced to NAM, and the blasphemous musical "Hair" with its anthem "Aquarius" was an enormous influence. Many of those young people who "dropped out" of society in the 1960s have long since "dropped" back into society, often holding influential positions, but still maintaining NAM ideas and forwarding its agenda.

## What It Is Not

NAM is not a cult in any traditional sense, as it has no recognised headquarters, no distinct governing body, no set creed or doctrinal statement of beliefs and no single organisational structure. Also it is not something restricted to a few muddy dropouts who are called "New Age Travellers" by the popular media. It is much more sophisticated and mainstream.

## What it is

NAM is a network of inter-connecting and overlapping organisations. It has been described as "not a bureaucracy or an organisation but a network of social and spiritual movements. Each is self-sufficient. Not one is essential to the whole, but NAM is becoming an evident source of potential power". This network reaches out into all areas of society, including alternative medicine, government, religion, music, diet, sport, education, films and entertainment, the ecology movement, industry, commerce, arts and publishing including Eastern and occult religious practices.

## Central Belief

The essential belief of NAM is that a new age is about to dawn, which will be called the "Aquarian Age".

This "golden" age will be a time when people realise their full potential and will be ushered in when enough people world-wide are "tuned in". This is very much a Hindu idea which requires a person's "individual consciousness" to be altered sufficiently to tune into the "universal consciousness". Anything can be used to help in altering the individual's consciousness, including drugs, hypnotism, yoga, meditation, scream therapy, brain-drive machines, sitting in pyramids, astral travel, occult activity, crystal use and many more. There are numerous doors into the mind-transforming world of NAM.

The Aquarian Age is named after the astrological symbol Aquarius, which is the water carrier and represents man's ability to carry his own load. Thus there is no need of God for in one sense man has become "god" and NAM is sometimes called "the deification of man". The Aquarian Age is said to supercede the age of Pisces which is the fish and also a symbol of Christianity. Thus NAM is a concerted effort to achieve a "quantum evolutionary leap" with humanity acquiring the attributes heretofore associated with God. This is the "consciousness revolution" with new ways of looking at and experiencing life, and when enough of humanity have entered this experience then a new age will have dawned.

Thus NAM is a blend of Eastern religious experience, occultic activities, psychic phenomenon and "me-ism". The latter simply means that there is a great emphasis upon "looking within" to find "the inner self" and develop "conscious awareness". It is often described as "selfism" and with obvious neglect of all others except "selfism" could easily be considered as "selfishism". The cement that holds this mishmash of ideas together is reincarnation. This is the Eastern idea of cyclic rebirth, where a person keeps paying for past misdeeds until the bad is balanced by good. The idea is that eventually the person atones for misdeeds and so the final redemption or absorption of the soul into the divine world soul (Nirvana) takes place. Indeed without reincarnation many would miss out on experiencing the new age!

This "new world order" is expected to have a one world army, government, police force, financial system and religion. It would seem that opponents will be eliminated, especially those who believe in Judeo-Christian truth. NAM rejects the God of the Bible for monism (that all is one) and pantheism (that all is god). Jesus is neither Saviour nor Son of God but an avatar or world teacher who helped to bring some spiritual enlightenment. Absolute truth is rejected and experiential subjectivism determines what is truth for the individual. NAM also denies the Biblical view of heaven and hell.

## Recognising NAM

Here are six indicators for identifying New Age activities:

1. A commitment to furthering the New Age, through unity of religions and uniting of national governments.

2. Belief in monism, pantheism, reincarnation, spiritual evolution, ascended masters, human potential and the essentially humanistic view that mankind is inherently good.

3. Occult activity such as channelling or mediumship, astrology, psychic healing, numerology, magic, induced states of consciousness, use of pyramids or crystals.

4. Use of terminology such as "higher self", "self-

realization", "cosmic consciousness", "universal energy", "chakras", "kundalini", "networking", "spaceship earth", "cosmic energy" and many more. Also the use of symbols such as rays of light, swastika, pyramid, triangle, eye in a triangle, yin and yang, rainbow and pegasus can indicate NAM involvement.

5. Certain political ideas such as "new world order" or "planetary citizen".

6. Today a lot of concern is rightly expressed over issues like health and the environment. Unfortunately, many approaches for dealing with these issues are under-girded by New Age philosophy. These include most aspects of holistic health, ecology-concerned parties and therapy groups such as "Forum", "Lifespring" and "Silva Mind Control" seminars.

It has to be said that committed New Agers are determined to usher in the Age of Aquarius, but many others are part of the New Age and unaware of it. They may have become involved through genuine concern for the environment, anxiety over their health or sadness at the loss of a loved one. Many are involved and do not believe all aspects of the New Age, indeed they may practice some New Age activities and be unaware of the central aims.

## Christian Witness

The Christian's approach needs to be:

1. **Prayerful**: Nothing is achieved and no New Ager can be led to salvation unless we keep close to the Lord and let Him lead us in our witness.

2. **Sensitive**: Most New Agers believe that Christians are harsh and uncaring. We must show the love of Christ and exercise great patience with New Agers who often have disturbed minds and can be in the grip of Satanic power. Therefore we must be careful

never to criticize or give the impression that we are in any way superior.

**3. Careful**: Here we must be deeply familiar with the Biblical truth we believe and show the evidence from Scripture and from personal testimony that the Gospel is both true and effective.

**4. Determined**: We must not give up either praying for New Agers or witnessing to them. This segment of society is particularly difficult to reach with the Gospel but we praise God that there are testimonies of those who have been delivered from the Satanic grip of the New Age Movement.

Christians should always be aware that it is easy to be dominated in our thinking by ideas from society as portrayed through the media. This influence is both subtle and powerful and can embed itself in us unconsciously. We need to search our hearts and minds and allow our ideas, values and beliefs to be shaped by the Lord, through His Word. We can then be in a position to become effective in our personal evangelism to those caught up in the New Age Movement.

# Final Word

The idea of this book is not to attack people or to call into question anyone's sincerity. It is simply an attempt to try and understand what the various religious movements believe and practice and to analyse some of the effects they have had on their followers. It is also designed to help the Bible believing Christian to be more effective in sharing the Good News of Christ with people who have been influenced by such movements. It is obvious that without some background understanding of another person's belief it is extremely difficult to understand them and to find a starting point for sharing the Gospel with them.

Certainly we as Christians do not come from a position of personal superiority, as we like everyone else are simply sinners, saved by the Lord through faith in Him. The result is that there radiates in our hearts the joy of Christ, brought about by the wonderful experience of forgiveness and we want to bring that delight to others by sharing the wonder of knowing Jesus Christ personally. We do not want to engage people in argument and certainly we must never be rude or offensive with those who see things differently from ourselves. All people should be treated with respect and dignity because the Saviour died for all mankind, because of His great love for everyone. We need to ask God for true sensitivity and a loving heart towards those who do need to hear about our Saviour.

However we must not present a vague message but one which is clear and Bible based. It is therefore so important to study and know what the Bible actually says about such things as the human condition, the prospect of judgment , the reason for Jesus' death, His powerful resurrection, the destiny of the human soul and the person of Jesus Christ. These are important issues and ultimately of vital concern to everyone. We need to understand such Bible teachings and then let the arguments of Holy Scripture be used to impress the importance of the Gospel upon others. It is always a blessing to encourage people to read the Bible for themselves, especially to do that prayerfully.

Let us always cloak our work with prayer. We need to be people of prayer as we engage in personal evangelism. It is good if other Christians join us in prayer to seek God's wonderful blessing and salvation upon those who might be caught up in the darkness of a false religion.

I hope that this small book will have stimulated some thinking and given insights into the whole area of religious movements and the need to evangelise those enmeshed in them. I hope that it has exposed the falsehood and the incorrect claims which many make and that it has made us more aware of the deep spiritual longing that exists in the human heart and the desperate search for truth in which so many are engaged. Bible believing Christians must not withhold the truth but share it and learn to be effective in demonstrating our faith for the benefit of others and the glory of the Lord Jesus.

# Bibliography

## 1. General:

*Understanding the Cults* by Josh McDowell and Don Stewart (Here's Life Publishers Inc.)

*New Religious Movement* by Eileen Barker (H.M.S.O.)

*The Secret World of the Cults* by Jean Ritchie (Angus and Robertson)

*The Kingdom of the Cults* by Walter Martin (Bethany House Publishers)

*Cults, World Religions, And You* by Kenneth Boa (Victor Books)

*Coping with the Cults* by Lorri MacGregor (MacGregor Ministries)

*What the Cults Believe* by Irvine Robertson (Moody Press)

*So What's the Difference* by Fritz Ridenour (Regal Books)

*Evangelising the Cults* by Ronald Enroth (Word Publishing)

*Examining the Cults* by Harold J. Berry (Back to the Bible)

*Cult Critiques* by Doug Harris (Reachout Trust)

## 2. Jehovah's Witnesses:

*Reasoning from the Scriptures with the Jehovah's Witnesses* by Ron Rhodes (Harvest House)

*Held by the Watchtower, set Free by Christ* by Susan Thorne (Crossway Books)

*The Jehovah's Witnesses' New Testament* by Robert H. Countess (Presbyterian and Reformed)

*How to Respond to Jehovah's Witnesses* by Herbert Kern (Concordia Publishing House)

*Awake to the Watchtower* by Doug Harris (Reachout)

### 3. Mormons:

*The Facts of Mormonism are stranger than Fiction* (Ed.) (Christian Information Outreach)

*The Twenty-Seventh Wife* by Irving Wallace (Four Square Books)

*Mormons* (Talking Points Publication)

### 4. Moonies:

*The Making of a Moonie* by Eileen Barker (Blackwell)

*The Locust Years* by Jacqui Williams (Hodder and Stoughton)

*The Rising of the Moon* by John Allan (IVP)

*The Moon is not the Son* by James Bjornstad (Bethany Fellowship)

*Heavenly Deception* by Chris Elkins (Kingsway)

*What do you say to a Moonie?* by Chris Elkins (Tyndale)

### 5. Christian Science:

*Christian Science* by A. A. Hoekema (Eerdmans)

*The Life of Mary Baker G. Eddy and the History of Christian Science* by G. Milmine (Baker Book House)

### 6. Central London Church of Christ:

*As Angels of Light* by Steve Wookey (Narrowgate Press)

*The 'Church' That's Brainwashing Britons* by Peter Browne (Reader's Digest, April 1994)

## 7. Scientology:

*Bare-faced Messiah* by Russell Miller (Sphere)
*A Look into Scientology* (Reachout Trust)

## 8. Islam:

*Understanding Non-Christian Religions* by Josh McDowell and Don Stewart (Here's Life Publishers)
*Understanding Islam* (Echoes of Service)
*Jesus Christ or Mohammed?* by F.S.Copleston (Islam's Challenge)
*McDonalds, Minarets and Modernity* by Bob Hitching (Spear)
*Cross and Crescent* by Colin Chapman (IVP)
*Ishmael My Brother* by Anne Cooper (Marc)
*The Principles of Religion in the Qur'an and the Bible* by Salim K. Haddad (Dorrance)

## 9. Occult:

*Paganism and the Occult* by Kevin Logan (Kingsway)
*The Occult and Young People* by Roger Ellis (Kingsway)
*The Satanic Revival* by Mark I. Bubeck (Scripture Press)
*Understanding the Occult* by Josh McDowell and Don Stewart (Here's Life Publishers)
*The Ouija Board a Doorway to the Occult* by Edmond C. Gruss (Presbyterian and Reformed)
*Satanism* by Bob and Gretchen Passantino (OM Publishing)

## 10. Astrology:

*Horoscopes and the Christian* by Robert A. Morey (Bethany House Publishers)

*What About Horoscopes?* by Joseph Bayly (Coverdale)

*The Facts on Astrology* by John Ankerberg and John Weldon (Harvest House)

*Today's Psychic Fayre* by Cecil Andrews (Take Heed)

## 11. New Age Movement:

*Understanding the New Age* by Paul Young (Echoes of Service)

*How to Respond to the New Age Movement* by Philip H. Lochhaas (Concordia)

*Gods of the New Age* by Caryl Matrisciana (Marshall Pickering)

*Inside the New Age Nightmare* by Randall N. Baer (Huntington House)

*Peace, Prosperity and the coming Holocaust* by Dave Hunt (Harvest House)

*The Hidden Dangers of the Rainbow* by Constance Cumbey (Huntington House)

*The Facts on the New Age Movement* by John Ankerberg and John Weldon (Harvest House)

*The New Age Cult* by Walter Martin (Bethany House)